A STREET LAMP
AND
THE STARS

A Street Lamp and
the Stars

The Autobiography

of

DON BORRELLI OF NAPLES

written with the help of

ANTHONY THORNE

COWARD-McCANN, Inc.   NEW YORK

Contents

Illustrations

Following page 64.

A STREET LAMP AND THE STARS

Now they know who I am I can walk
    among them as a priest

Their first Sacrament

Cooking under difficulties

First days in the Casa

Bringing in the scrap-iron

A pottery class in our first school

The joy of getting a present

Talking to *scugnizzi* in my office

All the photographs in this book were taken by my good friend Salvatore,
to whom I owe so much.

CHAPTER ONE

Double Exposure

The gesture betrayed me. The moment gave me away. It was a sudden incandescence in which I had unwittingly allowed my two lives to fuse together. It was dangerous, and it was intensely revealing. I had, I suppose, drawn a self-portrait without the aid of a mirror.

Fortunately, nobody saw me. The long Dominican corridor was deserted and silent, smelling of time and lit here and there in encouraging patches. But why on earth should a young priest, walking sedately in his soutane towards the cell of a friend—why should he suddenly dart forward into a shaft of light and stoop and scoop and snatch at some object on the grey flagstones?

As I straightened my back and looked anxiously over my shoulder I realised that it was because I was exhausted in body and brain, working all day at three jobs and nearly all night at a fourth, that I had allowed this to happen, or rather, had become incapable of preventing it. I have since learned to need no more than three hours' sleep, but at the beginning of my mission tiredness confused and drugged me, and my mind was no longer on guard. As I walked on again —a little more rapidly, to hasten away from the scene—I congratulated myself that at least this had happened only here, in a quiet spot, and that there were no witnesses.

I was lucky. I could easily have made the same gesture in view of all Naples—in a main street, the Via Roma, or the Via Caracciolo, outside the restaurant Zi' Teresa, or on the steps of the Tosca Cinema. People there would have been astonished and perhaps disgusted at such behaviour on the part of a priest, and at the worst I might have been recognised by some acquaintance as being Don Mario Borrelli. There would have been, to say the least of it, ex-planations to make; and I cannot tell you how tired I was of making explanations when my purposes were so simple.

My action had been simple too, automatic. Even if my brain had been clearer I could not at that moment have resisted doing what I did. For in nights of searching the gutters of Naples with my young vagabonds, my *scugnizzi*, I had never seen such a beautiful cigarette-butt.

Oh yes, a beauty. I can still think of it with tenderness. It was practically an unsmoked cigarette, and I believe it must have been thrown away in anger. (There was a Court of Assizes in the same building, and perhaps someone had just received a harsh sentence.) You will understand when you think of it how revealing and full of character a simple object like a cigarette-butt can be. Study it, and its former owner begins to take shape. Like my nights' companions I have become a connoisseur in such matters and can guess not only the mood of the smoker but the sex and sometimes the nationality too. Later on I shall have far more to say on the subject of cigarette-butts!

But that moment when a priest had stooped and grabbed instinctively was a moment of truth. There I was completely, and I can remember only one other comparable occasion— when somebody in a tram, who had been staring at me with an expression of horrified bewilderment, suddenly leant forward and plucked from my soutane a gaily cavorting louse which I had acquired the night before. I was so ashamed that I have never quite recovered. The incident of the cigarette-butt was at least less embarrassing, though at the time I was by no means amused. I cannot remember what my first reactions were—whether I was thankful that nobody wanted to fight me with fists or razor-blades for possession of my treasure trove—or whether I really wanted it for myself—or whether it was to have been a bargaining point in some transaction of the night—or whether, quite simply, I was ashamed as a priest of having behaved so indecorously.

Well, there it was; nothing to be done; and within seconds I was knocking on the door of my friend's cell.

A little later there emerged from it another character, and a very disreputable one. Torn and filthy old trousers patched like a map of Europe, a gaping and greasy shirt, a sweat-stained cloth cap pushed to the back of the head, ill-fitting boots which turned the act of walking into a painful and ugly shuffle—you might have reached in your pocket for a few *soldi* to stop the creature from bothering you, to get him out of your sight, to let you enjoy your good dinner without being reminded of poverty, to stop him from contaminating the sleeve of your jacket or the door-handle of your automobile. He might have stirred you to compassion, but you would never have trusted him with your baggage. He was— how shall we put it?—an uncomfortable presence, if not downright dangerous. Still, for services rendered, or because you cannot bear the sight of him any longer, his touting and pimping and fawning—you give him a few *soldi*. And you think that the matter is ended.

Just another of these *scugnizzi* (the word means, literally, "spinning tops") of whom, as you will learn later, there are many kinds.

Even if there *had* been a witness in that Dominican corridor, if he had noticed the incident of the cigarette-butt— I very much doubt he would have realised that the small slim cleric who went into that cell had anything to do with the scruffy lout who came lurching out of it.

But these two pictures—like twin, superimposed photographs on one piece of film—are of the same man, the "pocket priest" and the young tough from the back alleys or shanty-towns of Naples.

It is not merely that we seem to be the same; in many respects we *are* the same, it is as simple as that. Consider in any case how much we have in common : no place of our own, and yet every place our own; no material concern except for our everyday needs; no possessions to defend.

These things are as true of the one as of the other, and I would go so far as to say—indeed I have said it in the face of authority—that if a priest has nothing of the vagabond in him, then he is not a good priest.

However, authority did not at first agree. The complications, though we won in the end, were tremendous, unnerving, and at times quite infuriating. But again I anticipate, for there is so much to say.

So much indeed has already been said by others, who for various reasons have been pleased to describe in their own terms my life's work : which, briefly, is to rescue and protect the *scugnizzi*, the children of Naples who through no fault of their own have never had the time or opportunity to remain innocent. (Nor the *space*—that is important when you think of large families living in one room, even in one bed.) I had to put out my hand to these strange twilight creatures who are neither young nor adult and cannot be judged, nor even spoken to, as though they belonged to the one category or the other. Lost in a jungle, they have formed a category of their own; as a phenomenon they have existed through centuries, and from time to time efforts have been made to reach them, to help them. Only in recent years has their cause been publicised.

I am by no means ungrateful for this, for attention has been called to my House of Urchins, people in many countries have been moved by the story, and money—but never, never enough!—has reached us.

Perhaps I have been unwise to let others talk about Don Borrelli without opening my own mouth, but I have had so little time in which to tell my story. You cannot stand apart from the work that you desperately need to do, you cannot examine it clearly and dispassionately and record it on paper, for there the work is, waiting to be done. And another of my troubles was that I was forced to accept almost any offer of money that came to me, without thought of future possibilities, because of bills that came down like a snowstorm. (They still do.) Even a vision has to be paid for.

But at least that vision has been realised—the *Casa dello Scugnizzo* now exists and a second *Casa* will soon be built. And so for the first time, a priest of Naples most humble in matters of the spirit but most proud of my Neapolitan inheritance, I can tell you how all this has come about.

CHAPTER TWO

All this
to
Inherit

First of all I must give you some idea of what it means to be a true Neapolitan. For at least two centuries so much nonsense has been written about us that you would think we consisted entirely of indolent, beguiling rogues, ragged, picturesque music-loving pagans with ribboned mandolines, doting on our volcano. This image has been shaped for so long that, quite naturally, our own people have assisted in the process. They have deliberately exploited it, and surely that is understandable? Any shopkeeper, any waiter, any guide, would obviously rather please a stranger than criticise his judgment, even though in his heart he knows it to be exaggerated, even false. The Neapolitan is an actor in any case, and ready to play the part he finds written for him. (And if no part is written for him he will write it himself : observe the vivacious performance he gives in front of an unseeing telephone! As somebody recently said, it is only the bad actors in Italy who go on the stage.)

But then—what sort of people *are* we? You must give me a little time to tell you, for the answer is tremendous and also very complicated.

The word Naples itself means a new city—Nea-polis, which became Napule in our dialect—so it is obvious that the old one had had to be rebuilt. How old can it have been, one wonders? Near Santa Lucia there is a street called Via Palepoli (old town), which probably commemorates a Cuman city destroyed by the Greeks. Or was there some colony even older?

Who knows? Our roots are very deep in time and we flourish on its compost. Apart from the Greeks, Phoenicians came, Egyptians too, and Saracens with their plunder and rape and violence. And—though I say it with sorrow I cannot help smiling in sympathy, for I understand their problems—the *scugnizzi* must have assisted too. They were always there. At every disembarkation. Had there been national flags in those days, I feel sure they would have waved them. And pulled sailors by their elbows and told them where to go. And put up the price. Oh yes, they were always there : they lived by people who came from the sea, they always had. If Father Neptune had come ashore they would have done their best for him, and mislaid his trident.

Then, long after these invasions of the ancients, various

peoples arrived under the impression that they were con-
querors, whereas in fact we patiently absorbed them. These
were the Normans, the French, the Spanish, the Austrians,
fusing their blood with ours and making us what we are
today. And the *scugnizzi*, you can count on it, were always
there. It is indeed an historical fact that in front of every
regiment of invading troops there was always a band of
scugnizzi doing handsprings and cartwheels—how vividly
one can see it!—as though advertising a new circus just
come to town. Excitement? Maybe, but do you detect the
note of mockery?

After all that, and the handsprings and the cartwheels,
let us consider what we are today. We are Neapolitans, and
please take it from me that we are quite different, not only
in dialect but in feeling and in personality, from any others
of our countrymen. So much so that when people talk of the
Unification of Italy I simply have to laugh, for that was
merely an invasion of Italy by the Italians. Unification,
indeed! We of Naples are still Neapolitans.

But by the nature of things we are extremely complex
creatures inheriting diverse characteristics, some so much at
variance with others that it is hard to believe that they can
be present in the same person. Besides the creative impulse of
the Greeks you will find in us the sentimentality and
arrogance of the Spanish, a poor man's fatalism akin to
that of the Arab, the vivacity and quick-wittedness of the
Frenchman—and you will be confused by the mosaic of
our conflicting qualities. Sincerity and shrewdness, how do
they go together? And in what relation is indolence to
vitality?

17

(That word "indolence" in any case needs qualifying. A Neapolitan, providing that he is on his own, will work for himself and his family all day and half the night; but if he is working for the profit of others, if in fact his energy is being exploited, that is quite another matter and he is not nearly so anxious to bestir himself. As, of course, has been well noted by his employers and bitterly publicised.)

Yes, we are a puzzling people indeed, born on haunted stones and very well aware of our inheritance from the pagan world : and yet—I cannot say this too strongly—we are also a devotedly religious people for whom the Church is part of our daily life and absolutely inseparable from it. Of what other people can that be said?

There are so many other things to tell you! You know anyway that we cannot exist without music and that we are intensely proud that for two hundred years Naples was acknowledged by the whole of Europe to be its musical capital. Nowhere else were so many remarkable composers, singers, and *virtuosi* to be found—and their numbers increased as musicians from other countries came to join us. Many of them were distinguished, and their names still ring, but most of all that of Domenico Scarlatti (brought here by his father Alessandro), both composer and brilliant performer on the harpsichord, dazzling, ruminative, effervescent, witty—a true Neapolitan.

And you will find that even today, for any reason at all, for joy or for sorrow, because we are alone or because we are in company, because we are by the sea or on the sea or momentarily separated from it, we open our mouths and sing, or snatch up the nearest musical instrument—sometimes with a gaiety that will leave your ears ringing all night, and sometimes with a melancholy that is too profound for bitterness. (Do not be deceived, I beg of you, by the sugary vocalising that is nowadays accepted as being Neapolitan and exploited to the point of caricature. Can you really believe that it was on music of that sort that we made and maintained for so long our reputation as arbiters of musical taste in Europe?)

Then, after our music, our dialect.

That seems to me to follow naturally, but I suppose it will startle those who think our speech strange and uncouth and incomprehensible. Well, it is very much *del popolo*, and why should it not be of the people? It has richness, pungency and force, and if our voices sound odd to those unaccustomed to Naples, the fault is not ours.

What we speak is in fact a dialect deriving from the Pompeian version of Latin, and many words found on inscriptions in the ruined city seem far nearer to our everyday speech than to "standard Italian". But of course we have absorbed many foreign words too, as every language does that is a living language, and our tongue is spiced with Spanish and even salted with German—through the Austrians, who seem to have contributed quite a number of obscenities.

The Neapolitan speech can fall with devastating effect on the ear of one who is not expecting it. Since I have fair hair and blue eyes I am sometimes mistaken for an Englishman, and I remember once being approached by a station tout who wanted to sell me a wrist-watch.

"You give me five thousand lire?" he asked in English.

"Where I come from," I replied in the thickest Neapolitan, "we can buy them by the kilo for that."

You should have seen him jump.

By northern standards we are a most illogical people, and
I must tell you at once that there is nothing whatever to be
done about it. Our city provides cruel contrasts of magnificent sweeping views and fetid little alleyways, of huge
glittering hotels and shanty-towns of heartrending poverty
and squalor. And yet you would never manage to persuade
us that these large sums of public money spent yearly on
fireworks or on the fantastic electrical displays at the festival
of Piedigrotta (enormous changing pictures pricked out of
the night-sky by uncountable thousands of bulbs)—you
could never manage to persuade us that all that money could
ever be better spent. We know the arguments: that the
lives of the poor might be less miserable if it were diverted
to charitable uses, that there could be more schools too, more
hospitals, better housing. . . .

I see the foreigner's point of view. It is a shock for him
when he is watching a long procession of lavishly decorated,
gilded and floodlit floats moving slowly and majestically
down Via Chiaia, each one more fantastic and original than
the last—and at the same time an old man in rags, almost
too ill to beg, is trying to hold out his shaking hand: a skele-
ton at the feast indeed.

"Even one float less—and what could have been done
with the money?"

Yes, that is a logical point of view; but as I have said, we
are not a logical people. And besides, there is a good deal
more to be said about the matter.

You see, this is nothing whatever like the Battle of Flowers at Nice, or the Festival of San Remo. It is not designed to attract the tourist, it is a purely Neapolitan festival which brings not only pleasure and excitement into our lives but gives everybody, even the poorest, the chance of earning a little more. People vie with one another. Each of those magnificent floats was designed, made and contributed by a different quarter of Naples—and Naples has its many quarters. There is intense rivalry, too, among the shopkeepers, who try to outdo one another with their displays. This is not merely ostentation for the sake of ostentation; it is business instinct and it is also pride. Even the humblest can join in the game, and a little stall or a barrow knocked together from a few old boxes and transformed with a Neapolitan's gift for colour and design will be selling nuts or fruit or seeds, or sticky sweets, or paper hats and little gaudy frivolities.

And let me say it quite clearly: if there were no tourist in the whole of Naples at that time, the Neapolitan would do exactly the same. He is in any case forever celebrating— every vendor is always glorifying the street, for the street is part of his life.

Now a word about the Neapolitan on the defensive. He always fears and is suspicious of authority because it is something that from the beginning of time has been imposed on him by successions of invaders. He will therefore not react against it unless he thinks it will be really useful to do so— a champion of passive resistance. As to the police, he tries to avoid having anything to do with them. And he is on the defensive too if he leaves Naples for another town or country, deliberately losing his identity and trying to sink into the background of his new surroundings—a kind of protective colouring.

So there it is in brief—so much in brief that I wish there were time and space to say far more—an outline of the Neapolitan character. It is something in the air, in the light; one acquires it by inheritance or simply through the skin : by listening to the music of it and the sound of the sea —or indeed by the sound of the sea in the music! Hearing people sing. Hearing one's own voice in church. Walking in a city that is paved with volcanic stone. Out fishing in a breathing quietness, with a lamp to attract the octopus into thinking that it is a moon. Looking back, rocked and happy, at Naples standing there with terrace on lamplit terrace, and the floodlit Castel Sant' Elmo leaning out above us.

In our street cries too we are always hearing our Naples : the barrow-boys have a technique of calling out mockingly "Fruit!" when they mean "Fish!" and vice versa, and we all of us know exactly what is being sold. It is an accepted joke that they must advertise something quite different from what they are selling. And every street vendor's call has a cadence like a Gregorian chant.

Oh, there are so many things, and some even more difficult to define, that the children of Naples inherit and accept as part of their being. I use the word children because I do not only mean *scugnizzi*—our visitors are apt to think that any children seen on the streets, especially if they are in a group, are bound to be *scugnizzi*, which may not be the case by any means. Of children there are certainly many, but *scugnizzi* have their own reasons for being what they are.

22

I must point out too that not only Naples but her children, whether *scugnizzi* or not, have been horribly sentimentalised for a great number of years. Not only have their young faces and "picturesque" rags delighted so many painters and engravers, but even responsible writers like Norman Douglas have nauseated us with phrases like "the curly-pated little rascal" . . .

Let me tell you now of my own childhood, and you shall judge for yourself.

CHAPTER THREE

Early
Patterns—I

In 1922 I was born with, so to speak, a couple of masts and a funnel looking over my shoulder—in a district down by the docks, where my first cries must have vied with the sirens of arriving or departing vessels. In such a place one is always, always conscious of ships and the sea. They are part of the pattern.

It is a modest quarter, and even though it was badly bombed during the war, like so much dockside property, I still find that it has character, and that its charm for me is not merely that of familiarity. Its houses are old, but not particularly distinguished; just here and there, as in almost any quarter of Naples, one finds an unexpectedly pleasing architectural flourish. There is a fine stone arch on the ground floor of a balconied house in which I once lived, and as a boy I remember seeing two mules being led out of it. The coral-coloured plaster is patchy, but the sun makes it beautiful; and as the day goes on the sun drives the shadows in front of it, like dark sails going very slowly down the street.

The streets are cobbled. There is a square—one could almost have called it a village square—with a fine crucifix in the middle of it. And above all, our quarter (I seem to be reclaiming it for my own, though I left it long ago) has several shrines of quite exceptional beauty.

Perhaps the best of these is immediately opposite the house in which I spent most of my early boyhood. It is quite a large shrine and obviously very old indeed, a good example of early Neapolitan painting. The Madonna is at the same time primitive and tender in colour and line, and is set back from the frame by a broad fillet of finely wrought copper. On either side there are tapering marble pillars supporting a marble pediment.

In my childhood this beautiful Madonna had a silver crown, and there were real silver stars in the sky around her. During the war they disappeared—stolen, of course— and now the stars have been replaced by some glittering nonsense that really does not upset me as it would upset someone looking at the shrine for the first time, for I am seeing this Madonna with the eyes of a boy and the stars are still made of silver.

Silver. And now it is time to tell you that this is the quarter of the workers in precious metals, the small-scale jewel-

lers, the valuers, the fine craftsmen on whom the bigger shops
rely for skilful repairs and all manner of delicate operations
—a stone to be set in a ring, a gold chain to be shortened
or lengthened or mended, a splendid branch of coral to be
made into a brooch, a pair of antique earrings to be restored—they are the people, in fact, without whom the fash-
ionable jeweller, for all the glittering display in his window,
would be at a loss.

An intricate and very exacting work; and even at a late
hour in our quarter you can still see the craftsman in a lit
window, bent cautiously over some almost invisible link of
chain.

My father's trade was silver-gilding, and a brother of
mine worked with him. I myself, during my varied and
fidgety career as a boy, also lent a hand when other occu-
pations failed. Another brother was a jeweller. My sisters
and aunts were occupied in burnishing, which was considered women's work. Every one of us was somehow concerned with jewellery: we were properly of our quarter—
artisans in precious metal.

I was the youngest but one of five children, five more
having died in infancy or through miscarriages. Owing to
our small means, we had to take others into the house as
well—an aunt and uncle and a boy cousin, who were really
far more comfortably placed than we were. This boy was
well aware of the fact and, as boys do, lost no opportunity
of harping on it. He crowed over me incessantly, and since
our more modest position did not at that age appear to me
to be any fault of mine, I bitterly resented it.

Even now I have a rather quick temper and can explode

when angry: not unreasonably have I been nicknamed "Don Vesuvio", small though I am. As a boy I was of course far worse, and I am quite ready to admit that I fought and raged from morning to night and made everybody's life impossible. This bitter feud between my cousin and me penetrated to all corners of the place and occupied far too much of the conversation. Clearly it could not go on, it was driving everybody out of their senses. A solution must be found. Or even two if necessary.

Conclusion A. Little Mario must be given some sort of occupation that will distract him and keep him on the go and absorb all his energies.

Conclusion B. Little Mario could very well live away from this house—only a few doors away—but staying with a brother and sister who have taken a fancy to him. Then we shall all still be together, a family, but perhaps with this new arrangement we shall have a little peace at last . . . ?

So off went Little Mario, at the ripe age of eight, to a barber's shop—not to learn the trade, indeed, but just to fetch and carry. And when I still see little white-jacketed boys weaving through the streets and the menacing traffic of Naples holding small metal trays with cups of coffee covered with wet paper, I know exactly how they feel.

For this was what I had to do myself. "Mario, where are you? Go and fetch one white coffee, one black, and a glass of *anice*." Into the street I went.

Clients had to wait their turn for a shave or a haircut: and in Naples, if you cannot go to a bar, you make it come to you.

As for the brother and sister in whose house I was des-

tined to stay (though still under the wing of my parents),
I loved them because they were completely crazy, because
they let me run wild without questioning me, and because
from their terrace there was a view of the moon rising over
Vesuvius that can still make my spine tingle when I think
of it. I was rooted to that terrace, sharing it willingly with
a menagerie of cats, chickens and pigeons : but if other
children wanted to come on to it I forced them to pay toll.
So many sweets had to be given to me for the pleasure of
such a view.

On one side you could see the port of Naples and a con-
tinuous traffic of goods being taken to and from the ships—
taken then in carts, horse-drawn and with much noise : but
in that noise there was at least the sound of silver-belled
harnesses and iron shoes on the cobbles and the crack of
the whip and the voices of drivers greeting one another as
they came round the corner. (I think there is even more
noise today, but of a different quality; for now that port
traffic consists of grey anonymous lorries and trucks and
vans, and there is no longer anything to see or enjoy.)

The other side of the terrace gave a completely different
picture of Naples. Quiet streets and squares, fading colours,
shrines, the gentle quarter of the artisans. Crossing the terrace it was almost as though you went from one city to
another, and from animation and even turbulence to serenity.

On the terrace itself serenity was extremely rare, not
merely because of the resident livestock or of the children
imported by me, but because my demented foster-parents
made so much noise. The brother, who was nearly always

half-drunk, insisted on telling me the "facts of life" at the very top of his voice and even shouting sometimes to make sure that I understood what he was saying : and he never lost an opportunity of illustrating his thesis by lending me some indecent book that he had managed to pick up. Bemused with wine, he did not even notice the earthquake of 1930 and declared that we were all mistaken.

As for his sister, she too was quite capable of making a scene of dramatic proportions, and I remember her in one of her ungovernable rages even pulling the heads off chickens to emphasize the points of an argument in which she was involved. An energetic woman. Indeed I can now recall being dumped stark naked into a portable bath in which I was attacked with a scrubbing brush of the kind used on steps and floors.

I am not complaining. So often I made a deliberate nuisance of myself, even to the desperate extent of swallowing six coins and having to be shaken upside down with no result. And the six coins did not pay for the litre of oil that finally retrieved them. Oh, I was a dreadful boy, always hanging on the backs of trams and cars, always throwing stones at the fruit in the botanical gardens. But being crazy, these two people loved me : and I love them still.

*   *   *   *

Twice I worked for a barber. There was an interval in which I performed other functions, most of them insignificant but including, of course, the family trade of artisan-jeweller. However, after four years I ended up, as though it were an *aria da capo*, in a second barber's shop. Snip, snip and scrape again, and the smell of lather and towels.

It was there that I met Don Nobilione, a priest whose influence imposed on the meaningless divagations of my childhood the beginnings of a pattern. I used to watch and wait for his arrival so that I could speak to him again, and if for any reason he did not appear when I thought he should I was so rude to everybody else that I had to be put in my place.

The most important conversation I ever had with him took place on a day that began disastrously. Early that morning the barber sent me to fetch three coffees from the bar down the road and on the way back, not looking where I was going, I walked straight into a letter-box jutting out from the wall. Up went the coffee, down went the cups, and my white jacket was no longer white. Whimpering with rage and mortification I turned and went back, not to the brother and sister, but to my mother herself, since it seems to be a law of Nature that only mothers can deal with childhood's misfortunes.

She took in the situation with one glance, expressed her opinion of it with two slaps, tore off my jacket to plunge it into water, found me a clean one, and told me to blow my nose.

Chastened, though still far from calm, I went back to Haircuts and Shaves, explained what had happened, and found that Don Nobilione had arrived in my absence and was already receiving attention.

We smiled at one another in the glass and I made up my mind to speak to him before he left. For I had something very important to say, something I had never yet said aloud, something I had kept in my heart. And if it had not been for the absurd episode of the spilt coffee, the slaps and the emotional upheaval (always exaggerated in childhood) I would probably not have been able to open my mouth or know exactly what it was that I wanted to say.

I took his hat from the peg, brushed it, and stood waiting with it. It seemed a long time before he got up.

"Father, I want to be a priest."

I could not say firmly "I am *going* to be a priest", for how was this possible for a barber's boy whose parents had very little money?

Don Nobilione looked down at me gravely and I wondered what he was going to say. He could so easily have said: "Are you sure, my son?" But all he said was:

"Then you will need to go to school."

The implied acceptance of the situation was like music to me.

"Yes, I know."

"And what does your mother say about it?"

Then the music suddenly stopped, for I had not told her. And I knew in any case that my parents could hardly afford to educate me.

He must have seen me looking downcast, and he must have guessed the situation, for he put his hand on my shoulder and said quietly:

"Shall we tell her together?"

"When, tonight?"

For a boy of thirteen, things that are important have to be done *at once*. Suspense is impossible.

Don Nobilione smiled.

"Very well, my son. Tonight."

I told him where they lived, and he nodded and went away without another word.

Music again—and I suppose it should have been *Figaro*. For if in the barber's shop they had said to me *"Mario qui! Mario qua!"* I would have run about with delight.

*   *   *   *

My dear mother shook her head. The whole idea was a shock to her in the sense that she had never envisaged the possibility, and she could not in any case imagine that the possibility existed. I suppose I had managed things very badly in being so precipitate, especially after my performance that morning, but in youth one is less than diplomatic. I should have told her beforehand, but somehow I could not even mention Don Nobilione's visit until he was already on the stairs.

"No, I am afraid not . . . no, but how could Mario—? Then, the schooling, yes I understood about the schooling, but you see . . . no, how could we possibly afford it?"

There seemed to be no way out. But at least the discussion went on long enough for my mother to absorb this new and startling fact, that I wanted to become a priest. It was not that she disapproved, but she kept wondering how it could possibly happen. (And remembering the earlier Mario, she might even have thought it a trifle out of character!) In any case, there was always this terrible question of money.

32

It was then that Don Nobilione startled us both.

He would pay for everything, even for my books, and I would go to the Apostolic School for Boys.

If I did not thank him adequately then—I think I was too overwhelmed to do so—I have been trying to thank him ever since for his faith in me.

As things turned out, however, the matter of my schooling was not so easily settled. After the first year Don Nobilione, himself a poor man, could not afford to carry on any longer—and there were still four more years to go! Was that first year to be wasted?

My mother, by now convinced that I really meant to be a priest, that I was quick to learn and that my teachers approved of me, herself worked to find money to continue what Don Nobilione had begun. It was a terrible strain for her, and a strain for me too, for the money was never enough. I was absolutely obliged, in such a situation, to become top of my class and to stay there: had I lagged behind I would never have been allowed to remain.

But at the same time I was often without books. I had to borrow them—never, of course, for long enough—and learned to absorb the largest amount of information in the shortest possible period. Memory-training became an essential part of my studies, and sharpened my wits: and circumstances forced me into the strictest self-discipline.

As for my clothes—and how much aware I was of winter and summer!—they became thinner and shabbier and more mended. My shoes I had to repair myself, and I remember doing so with the brass wire that my father used for dipping metals into an acid bath.

Difficult years, full of pain and sacrifice, and not only for me. But I say this to you, Don Nobilione, that I would go through them time and time again for the sake of being admitted, as I was in 1940, at the age of eighteen, into a seminary.

I had a great deal to learn, although cigarette-butts were not yet on the curriculum. That was, shall we say, a post-graduate course.

And in the meantime—war.

CHAPTER FOUR

Early
Patterns—II

I have never regarded a soutane as being the most suitable garment in which to play football. The game demands less clothing rather than more. And on my very first day in the seminary, when the ball bounced away and I climbed over some iron railings to retrieve it, I became involved and impaled and split my cloth from end to end. It took me a little while, in fact, to get accustomed to wearing the thing. But how ironical that seems when I think how, in later years, I felt completely lost when I put my soutane aside in order to disguise myself. It was like losing my skin.

The Seminario Maggiore di Capodimonte seemed vast to me at first—a great palace with flights of marble staircases and endless curving corridors, six dormitories, a big library, classrooms in which the last words of lecturers seemed always to be vibrating, a chapel, and a long refectory on three sides of which were white marble tables ready to feed at least a hundred and twenty. There was also a big semicircular terrace with a magnificent view—away out to sea, over the port, and then to your right the mounting houses of the hilly Vomero quarter. How beautiful at first, this terrace; but how much less beautiful later, when one could watch from it all too easily the bombing of Naples.

And, as I suppose inevitably happens, the vastness diminished with growing familiarity.

One's own particular class is always, of course, by far the most interesting, and always contains the greatest number of "individuals". It is one of youth's more forgivable platitudes. Proximity gives you the greater chance of studying your fellows, a temporary monopoly of the microscope. Not that you are consciously clinical about such matters. You just see and accept people and form quite inexplicable attachments, later perhaps to be dissolved and quickly forgotten—still later to be remembered with astonishment or with pleasure.

There were twenty of us, and I think I can say truthfully that we were boys of all possible moods and kinds and backgrounds, a good cross-section of humanity. And yet in spite of being so diverse we must have contrived to give an impression of forming a united front, for we became known to the rest of the seminary as "the bunch of grapes", so much did we seem to hang together. All our misdeeds were designed and carried out by us as a body, and we suffered collective punishments—by far the severest of which was to be for-bidden to speak to our families for long periods.

Like all high-spirited students, we were eternally organ-ising "rags" of one sort or another, buffooneries which are never quite as funny in retrospect as they were at the time. That old favourite the mock lecture was duly arranged, though the hoax was discovered before the "lecturer" was far advanced in his discourse. I myself took part in an absurd burlesque designed to make fun of our Vice-rector, who was as tall as a monument. Standing on the shoulders of a friend, with a long black cloak draped over us, I was announced as "a visitor to the seminary" and was ushered into a wait-ing room with brown leather armchairs and a chandelier. Unfortunately my lower half had forgotten the need for peepholes and plunged blindly on, whilst I, holding my hand out in greeting, fell over backwards. But for one moment the Rector thought he had met someone even taller than himself.

We of course had our own college of cardinals and elected our own Pope. I remember that we enthroned him on a very high chair, to which he would never have climbed if he had realised that we were about to let off firecrackers underneath it. And on another occasion I put fifteen lizards in our Pope's bed. (I caught them on that semicircular sunlit terrace, and they are not as difficult to catch as you might think. Never try to take them by the tail. Make a little noose on the end of a twig, and you will have them by the head.)

"Our Pope's being eaten by crocodiles!" we shouted, as he leapt shrieking from his bed. "We must elect a new Pope at once!"

If such juvenile high-jinks seem silly or shocking to you, even sacrilegious, I suggest that they are really part of a perfectly harmless psychological process. The seminarist is bringing into his ordinary daily life the things which he loves and reveres. It is not mockery, though it may seem so. He is concerned with making holy things familiar, even part of his jokes, whereas for the layman they must always be on a different plane, barely accessible.

Another thing to remember in relation to our buffooneries is that we were soon in the midst of war, with bombs falling all round us and the walls of the seminary shaking and our windows blown in on us—a time in which laughter was apt to become a trifle high-pitched.

From the long windows (glassless of course) that led to the terrace I saw with horror the bombing of Naples and the crumbling of so many buildings that had been part of our landscape. Why weren't we hit? It seemed like a game of noughts and crosses with us as the centre. I hated seeing it, and yet could not keep away from the spectacle. I was terrified : and I remember discovering the fact that one can reduce fear by eating, even if it is only a small crust of bread. I watched, and I ate what I could find to eat. But even then fear sometimes got the better of me, especially when German tanks started shelling us and when there were pitched battles in our grounds between Germans and Italian patriots.

From time to time we had no water and were forced to drink from the fishpond under the semicircular terrace. Surprisingly, it did us no harm. As for food, it was in very short supply and we were eternally hungry at a time when one needs sustenance more than ever in one's life.

38

I remember our tall Vice-rector—a taciturn man who was at first unpopular but who gradually won our affections until we loved him—taking chestnuts out of his deep pockets and explaining to us (he was also a Professor of Biology at the University) the number of calories contained in each one, and as we slowly and solemnly ate what he gave us I am sure that his explanations helped to make those chestnuts a little more sustaining. But at the various tables at which I sat, for as time went on we progressed from one to another, we seemed to be living mostly on laughter.

* * * *

The scream, the flash, the shudder of the earth under you. But why should this bomb, more than any I had seen fall on Naples, seem to tear something out of my inside?

I turned and ran distractedly down the corridor. The Vice-rector stopped me.

"Where are you going?"

"That last bomb—it fell on my house!"

"How do you know? Did you see the address on it?"

Earth shuddered again, but without affecting me as it had before. I looked up at the Vice-rector.

"I knew where it went. Down by the docks. Behind the Via Marina. On my house. Perhaps on my parents."

He touched me on the shoulder and said quietly:

"Are you sure your parents were there?"

No, I could never be sure of that. My father, a most improvident man, was often incapable of paying the rent and in my earlier days there had been many removals. You could never be quite certain where they were living.

Again there was a bomb-shudder. I said :

"They were living there when I last heard from them."

"When was that?"

"A month ago."

"By now they could be anywhere."

"But they could also be dead under that house."

The Vice-rector's hand tightened on my shoulder for a moment. Then he said calmly :

"And if they *were* dead—what could you do?"

How cold the words sound as I repeat them, and on paper they look almost inhuman. But they were the words of a wise and sensible man and they did what he required them to do.

I turned away and went into the chapel.

The next morning my sister and brother-in-law came to see me. My sister was obviously suffering from shock—staring beyond me, her eyes too full of what she had seen the day before, and telling me what had happened in repetitive phrases. My brother-in-law steadied her.

"Mother and father?" I asked anxiously.

"Alive," he said. "But how did you know what had happened, up here in Capodimonte?"

"I can't tell you. I saw it—felt it—what does it matter? Were you all in a shelter?"

"No time. We were out in the streets, lying in the gutter." He put his arm round my sister. "We must go now, because of the lorry."

"The lorry?"

"Yes, we're being sent out of Naples with a lot of other families. So many people are going—with or without transport. We're lucky. But you can imagine what the roads will be like!"

My sister flung her arms round me.

"*Ciao*, Mario, *ciao!*"

Then they were suddenly going before I had quite understood what was happening. I called after them :

"But *where*? Where are they taking you?"

My brother-in-law turned back at the door.

"To Valva," he said, and they were gone.

Valva? It meant nothing to me, I had never heard of it. Valva could have been near Venice or in the toe of Italy. As soon as I could get into the library I managed to find it on the map—a small place in Calabria, beyond Eboli. (Five hundred metres high, surrounded by mountains, and with over two thousand inhabitants.)

Not so far, after all. My relatives would of course be taking the main road to Salerno. . . .

And almost the next day the Salerno landings burst on us like a dam—American and British forces bombing and shelling and shattering and maiming and scorching. I often wondered what fine principles could have justified this chaos, and if they would ever be upheld when order was finally restored. But as I said, we Neapolitans have known suffering before, and it is just as well that we have.

Still, I was tormented. The very road on which my family would be travelling was suddenly the focal point of the war's fury. Could they have got through in time? They would have been taken by lorry or truck as though they were cattle, and normally they would have been able to reach Eboli at least before the inferno began—but how slow might their progress have been on roads blocked by refugees from Naples?

Days passed without any news at all, and I could bear it no longer. They had gone in a fatal direction : it would almost have been better if they had stayed in the city. But I must go and find them in—where was it, Valva?—and make sure that they were still alive. And this time the Vice-rector agreed, realising perhaps that though I was hot-headed I was also deeply in earnest and that what I wanted to do I must do. He let me go.

From Capodimonte I started to run down to the port—stupidly, for I should have tried to reserve my energies at the beginning of the journey; but I had no idea of what that journey would involve, and I was far too worried to be able to steady my pace.

Down in the dock district I found myself crunching broken glass under my feet and climbing over piles of rubble that other footsteps had turned into bridges : you did not walk past houses now, but over them. In one moment of panic I did not even know where I was, for outlines were no longer familiar. Eventually—yes, that must have been where our house had stood. The beautiful shrine, without glass but not even scarred, gave me my bearings.

And then, with no money in my pocket and no food with me I started on a journey that even with occasional lifts was to take me three days.

The road was black with people from Naples pushing hand-carts or even perambulators and street-barrows on to which they had piled their few remaining possessions, and in the opposite direction booted American soldiers were marching towards the city. The verges were piled high with empty shell-cases. There were even live ones here and there, and I had to shout at children to stop playing with them.

Torre Annunziata . . . How easy it had been to run my finger over the map and decide what route I should take, but in hours and hours of walking I seemed to have achieved so little. Gratefully I accepted a lift in a small donkey cart whose owner was probably startled and curious at the sight of a small and extremely dusty priest walking determinedly away from Naples. He shared his meal with me—beans and apples and a swig of wine. Beans and apples were all that I was ever given on that journey—indeed the only food that seemed to exist during those days—but they were always handed to me with an air of accepting rather than of bestowing a favour. (Typically Neapolitan, that: no man, however poor or hungry, could bear to eat his food in your presence without at least asking your permission, even your blessing, and more likely than not he will ask you to share it with him.)

That first night I spent in a *cantina*—a small wine-shop —in Pompeii. It was crammed with refugees from Naples, cocoons of men, women and children lying closely together all over the floor. The sight of them, and the idea of sleeping among all those people embarrassed me: and if that sounds squeamish do please remember that in those days I was still the young seminarist, strictly brought-up and bashful even about my everyday bodily functions. Prudishness of that sort I was soon forced to forget—and of course to repudiate entirely when I later became a vagabond. But at that time it was still strong in me, and only utter exhaustion could persuade me to lie down with people of both sexes in one happy snoring family, a sort of communal bed.

Then on to Nocera Superiore, and between there and Salerno I was given—or rather, stole—another lift.

This time it was in an American truck driven by an enormous negro with very broad shoulders and the rather surprised expression that negroes sometimes have. The truck had stopped because of a minor accident: while it was parked by the roadside an officer's car had backed into it. No great damage and no trouble, but during the discussion that followed I heard the word "Salerno", and decided to be a passenger. I was glad anyway to get into the shade and I jumped up before anyone could see me.

Discussion over, slam of door. Engine reluctant, muttering of negro. Door opened. Bonnet opened. Pause. Bonnet slammed, door slammed, reluctant engine. Negro muttering. Sudden frog-like leap which nearly threw me back on to the road, and away we went.

Not a very comfortable journey, but I was in no position to complain. And the least comfortable part of it was when the truck was stopped just outside Salerno by the U.S. Military Police. I heard the shouts but could not at first understand what they meant. Nor can I very well remember what was said, but to my Italian ears it sounded something like this :

". . . twunnyfour cases to Naples, Sarge, then Ah have to come way back to Salerno." (The negro's voice sounded extraordinarily high to me, for a man so enormous.)

"O.K. So you come right back from Naples to Salerno

44

and you got nothing in your truck. And you think you can fool me."

"In that truck Ah don't bring nothin', Sarge, Ah don't bring nothin'. You go see for yourself Ah don't bring nothin'."

Crunch crunch of feet, shuffle and crunch. It would be any moment now. The canvas was lifted, two faces peered, and there was I smiling politely.

"Well—just imagine. You got nothing in your truck, you peanut, you gotta *priest*!"

The negro, looking more surprised than ever, stared at me with huge eyes and then I saw his mouth twitch.

"Well anyway, Sarge", he said, "it's only a *little* priest!"

At that we all burst out laughing. The sergeant tossed his half-smoked packet of cigarettes to me, the negro gave me a match and a blazingly white smile, and down we went past Vietri into ruined Salerno.

*   *   *   *

From Salerno I had to cut inland to Battipaglia and it was somehow difficult for me to leave the sea. I felt as though I were walking right off the map as we know it and into some mythical country on ancient charts. I spent the second night in a church full of refugees with opposite intentions—some who had left Naples, and some who could not do anything but return to it.

Then the next day to Eboli. It was getting harder and harder to walk and here, where I most needed a lift in some vehicle, none approached me that was not already piled high with goods or people or both. I remember knocking at the door of a house to ask for water and being offered wine—for which I would have been grateful if only I had had more to eat, but water it must be, even after another meal of beans and apples, or I would never be able to reach Valva. Eating, I caught sight of my face in a mirror once and was startled. I looked nearly as black as my friend the negro, for sweat and bomb-dust had combined to put a mask on me, a kind of dark pastry.

My third night's rest was in a stationary train, in company with people who were sleeping all over it, even in the baggage-racks. Most of them were waiting for the train to start in the morning and I longed to go with them, for it would have taken me to a place called Contursi, far nearer to Valva. But I had no money to pay for my ticket, so I had to climb down on to the track and watch the train going away from me; and then plod slowly after it.

Slowly and more slowly . . . As I said, Valva is about five hundred metres above sea-level, but to me it became a mountain. That last lap, from Contursi to Valva, took me four hours.

And then, at the very last moment, I failed. So much tiredness, emotion and hunger—my feet would not do what I told them to do and I stumbled and the world began going round very quickly . . .

I woke up in a real bed, clean, with my parents and relatives round me and full of affection.

"But if you'd only seen your face!" said my sister. "It was black. You looked almost like a negro. Oh, how you'd have laughed!"

For about a month I stayed with them.

*　　　*　　　*　　　*

The return journey seemed easier and quicker, as is so often the case with return journeys. I made it in company with many others who had previously been sent out of the city, for Neapolitans (like the Cockney Londoners, I am told) could not help returning to the place they loved, even at the risk of being killed there. Back they must go: and I too, with the added reason that I was long overdue in Capodimonte and would have to work extra hard to catch up with my studies.

My sister and brother-in-law came with us, impelled by the same homing-instinct, and at some point in the journey I lost them both. This not only worried but starved me, for they were carrying our food, such as it was. (The situation resolved itself, for I heard from them both a few weeks later and in the meantime people shared what they had with me.)

But where did I lose those two? It was probably during the episode of the empty truck.

Yes, a large truck or lorry carrying nothing whatsoever was purring contentedly on its way towards Naples. The stragglers in our party yelled at us in the front to stop it, and stop it we did, clambering all over the driver. He was an Italian, I am ashamed to say, and he refused to take us with him. What would he get out of it? (Be merciful to him, for that was the prevailing attitude of the time.) And the combined resources of our party could only have produced a few miserable *soldi*.

I resolved the problem and I led the charge. The bashful seminarist of a month ago reverted to Mario the Militant and vaulted up into that truck followed by at least twenty or thirty others, all shouting with anger.

This was *Borrelli's Little War*. I could not bear the idea of that driver bowling happily over all those kilometres with an empty truck behind him and all of us on our dusty feet.

He never stopped complaining, of course, sometimes taking both hands from the wheel for what seemed like several minutes. The only valid argument he produced was that if a bomb or shell hit the truck we would all of us be blown to the sky, whereas if we were walking on the road we would be dispersed and able to take shelter.

But our answer to that was a typically Neapolitan one. We started singing.

*   *   *   *

Only when I was before the Vice-rector did I remember to look at my soutane. You can imagine what it was like.

*   *   *   *

I was in the seminary for seven years, during the last three of which a young man called Ciccio become my greatest friend. We were an unlikely pair, he calm and serious and I as mischievous and energetic as a monkey; and my influence on him was not one that contributed to law and order. I remember egging him on to climb the trees in the gardens of the *seminario* and pick the fruit, which was strictly forbidden. Contrary to popular belief the stolen fruit was rather nasty, but we were glad of it all the same.

Ciccio—now Don Spada—was in some way which I still do not understand destined to become involved in my life. It is not enough to say that our sympathies were the same; that we had the same ideals, that we thought in the same way. Even when we lost contact with one another—as happened later—we were, inexplicably, travelling on parallel lines. By instinct we were dedicated to the same ends, and when I look back I am astonished to think how much we were complementary to one another. There would have been far less waste of effort if we had stayed together from the beginning.

But enough of Ciccio for the moment: he will help me later on. And enough of war too. Although I am by no means indifferent to the criminal folly of it, I am a man of Naples for whom waves and successions of invaders are part of history. It was not by any means the first time that we had been fought over or that we had known violence and death. We are a very ancient people.

No, it was the *aftermath* of war that horrified me more than the war itself. The by-products are incredibly evil: granted an open license to kill his fellow human beings— indeed encouraged to do so and rewarded for it—a man seems to be corrupted to the very roots of his being. Once murder becomes "respectable" where does he stop? And why should he stop? Why shouldn't every hidden desire be given full rein? Steal. Go on the Black Market and make yourself rich. Indulge your body as you like and as often as you like. Almost anything you can think of is yours for twenty cigarettes or a small tin of ham. These Neapolitans are starving. This is your chance. You'd be a fool if you didn't. Everybody else is doing it, so why not you?

As for the *scugnizzi*—they prospered as never before, assisting enthusiastically in every racket or vice that could bring them a few *soldi*. If our invaders found a situation from which they could profit, so did the sharp urchins. Those welcoming handsprings and cartwheels paid enormous dividends. Some American negroes were even "owned" by various *scugnizzi* who supplied them with what they wanted at tremendous profit and were prepared to hire them out, for another day, to other *scugnizzi*. It is even said that one *scugnizzo*, on the turnover from American negroes, managed to buy himself a small house outside Naples.

Such was the festering world into which I emerged as a priest in July 1946. It did not really surprise or shock me, but it hurt me deeply and I knew that something had to be done.

In the meantime I had plenty to occupy me, having taken on no less than three jobs at once.

A facility for languages had made me a member of the Holy Year Committee—in the seminary I had studied Spanish, German, and English, and had in fact been instrumental in saving the huge building, with its six dormitories, from being turned into a hospital. The Germans wanted it, then the Americans, then the English (who were far more stubborn than any). Acting as interpreter between the superiors of the seminary and the generals, I had managed to convince the latter gentlemen after much argument that the seminary was Vatican property and was therefore not to be touched. There is no better way of learning a language than by being faced with the really urgent necessity for speaking it! I do not now remember what I said, but the fact that I could make myself reasonably clear in English had not passed unnoticed by the authorities.

As for my other jobs, I was a schoolmaster; and I was also a travelling chapel. That is to say, I had acquired an ancient Austin ambulance van, a real rattler, in which I drove out into the suburbs in the chilly hours before dawn, hearing confessions and saying mass for the factory workers before they began their day. It was, of course, more than one could expect of their employers to allow them ten minutes off in which to go to church. Very well, then, the church would come to them, smelling more of petrol than of incense.

Then something else occurred to me. If I could reach the workers I could reach their children too—these small restless creatures with large eyes whom curiosity drew towards my van. So far from being able to ignore them, I was delighted by them. They smiled at me and I smiled back and we laughed at one another, and small hands were lifted to me in welcome or farewell. Our relationship did not need establishing, it had always existed. For any Neapolitan is a second father to every child he sees.

A puppet show, that was the answer. I could put a proper puppet show into my van, worthy of Naples and with the familiar figures of the *Commedia dell'Arte*, striped, patched and grotesque. Pulcinella would be taught how to make the sign of the cross, and his friends would be learning their catechism. The children would laugh—and they would learn too. They would come to me for amusement, carrying their smaller brothers and sisters, and they would take something away with them. I wish you could have seen all those large dark eyes, and the white smiles of pleasure.

This was, I suppose, my very first experiment in bringing our church into everyday life. Let it become part of the laughter that is so necessary to us all, let it be real, even a sacred joke.

I was beginning to learn how to reach people.

CHAPTER FIVE

Dress Rehearsal

The patterns of my life were not of my own making. They kept arranging themselves at unexpected times and in unlikely places. Even when I went on a peaceful holiday to a camp in a mountainous region called Matese, north of Naples, I became involved in a difficult situation from which I was able to learn a great deal.

Far above us, at a height of some eighteen hundred metres, there was a community of *carbonai*—the lonely hardworking charcoal-burners, whose trade, as they themselves know, is slowly dying. Years ago charcoal was used a great deal for cooking, especially in places where there was little wood to be obtained; but nowadays the gas cylinder has found its way into even the poorest houses and charcoal is today used only for heating.

Working for ten, twelve, even eighteen hours—from morning to night—these families live under the most wretched conditions, building themselves temporary houses of straw, wood and clay, and sleeping on heaps of leaves. They have no amenities whatsoever, and nobody gives them a thought, even when they are ill. Indeed, they are generally despised and disliked by villagers, rather in the same way as gypsies are frowned upon in England; a strange lot they are, with white eyes and very white teeth in smoke-black faces; ragged, uncouth, forever hungry and thirsty; leaving areas of devastation behind them, moving from one place to another, one tree to another, and owning nothing but a few horses and some battered pots and pans.

Such are the charcoal-burners, a people condemned to poverty, isolation, ignorance, and the contempt of their fellow men. Try to imagine the psychological effect of their condition, and think how you yourself would set about getting to know them.

Once a month they had to come down into the valley for their provisions—and in their simplicity they were always cheated by unscrupulous shopkeepers. They also had to fetch from below many barrels of water to extinguish their burning mounds of wood—each one like a miniature Vesuvius, the airholes smouldering with small branches because they burn the quickest, and the whole mound taking at least forty hours to turn into charcoal.

And so they arrived, grimy ragged men on a train of horses led by a grey mare. If I had been dressed as a priest when I first saw them we could never have spoken, for they were all of them, as you can well imagine, ardent communists. (I remember their referring to Togliatti as "*he of Rome*"!) But I was dressed in ordinary practical clothes suitable for mountaineering, and perhaps they were surprised to find somebody ready to laugh and joke with them. How white the teeth seemed in those black faces, and how good it was to see them bared in amusement!

I went up to their miserable camp in the mountains, a journey of about three quarters of an hour, and I took them tins of food and biscuits. And when one of them was sick I brought medicine. We became friends during that month in Matese and they developed the habit of sending down for me every day that dear and sensible beast, the grey mare. No saddle, of course, and one had to hold on by her mane or else fall off. She was ponderous, careful and grave, and she understood her duties and her place in the scheme of things. There was never a moment's argument. I think the charcoal-burners must have found some way of talking to her. She knew that she had to come down to fetch me and then bring me back. It was as simple as that. The *carbonai* had become my friends and were no longer shy of me; and their good beast and I understood one another.

They thought of me as an ordinary camper, of course—I was, so to speak, "disguised" as a mountaineer, and they had absolutely no idea that I had anything to do with the church.

But one Saturday afternoon—I could not hold myself back any longer—I begged them to come down into our camp the next morning, to hear mass. I suppose they were surprised at first, and a little doubtful, but some of them, perhaps to humour me and because I had shown them friendship, agreed.

They arrived on that Sunday morning, and it was unnerving—so many of them, so many more than I had imagined—and for the first time they saw me as I really was, a priest in his vestments, saying mass.

Then, after mass, they got back quietly on to their horses, and went up and away into their mountains without a single word . . .

That afternoon I was miserable. I felt I had handled the situation so badly—I had merely bought their affection with my little tins of food and my biscuits and my medicines and my jokes. They would never trust me again. I had not even had the courage or the honesty to tell them that I was a priest.

But then—supposing that I had done so—how would they have reacted? I might have won their friendship in the end, but my task would have been infinitely harder : they would have been convinced that I was an ally of their employers and that I really cared nothing for them— whereas I loved them so much. They would even have edged away from me, thinking that I was some kind of spy.

Was it right for me to have disguised myself, or was it wrong? I desperately needed an answer.

The answer came slowly down the path towards our camp, that placid grey mare gravely nodding her head. They had sent her to fetch me as usual.

I leant against her warm flanks and wept with relief. It was all right, and I was still their friend. Never shall I forget the feeling of that coarse strong mane in my fingers, almost cutting them, and the human heat of her ribs on the insides of my knees. She took me back to the *carbonai*, and in this afternoon light the mountains had never looked so splendid.

*   *   *   *

Back in Naples I had my three jobs waiting for me, and of course I had to find myself a fourth—a youth club on the lines of *La Jeunesse Ouvrière Catholique*. I could not stop. I wanted more and more work, I had so much energy and it did not seem ever to have found its proper outlet. I was forever nagging the authorities. Finally our parish church of Materdei allowed me to turn a small subsidiary church (S. Gennaro a Materdei) into a centre for our youth club, and that certainly needed plenty of helping hands. It was not only decrepit, it was even structurally dangerous— I am sorry to say that there are many Neapolitan churches in exactly the same state—and we had considerable difficulty in making it habitable and safe, to say nothing of its being made presentable.

This was not enough, it was never enough, the work I was doing. I seemed to be lunging out in so many directions without any clear sense of where I was going. Oh, one can be useful in so many ways, and there is always something to be done in this world—but how do you ever discover where your centre really is? In fact, what you yourself mean, what you are, why you are just that person, and what you intend to do? If you have always been clear about such matters I must congratulate you, but frankly it took me a little while to discover what my life's work had to be.

It was becoming increasingly clear to me that it was the *scugnizzi* whom I really wanted to help. Everything that one heard and saw of them was horrifying, and their numbers did not seem to be diminishing. The authorities were completely apathetic about this problem : bands and gangs of homeless children roaming the streets of Naples all night meant nothing to them at all. There were hundreds and hundreds of these urchins, many of them vicious—and many of them extremely dangerous.

What could I do for them? And what could I possibly hope to do *alone*?

Again I asked for an answer; and again it came.

*   *   *   *

A prosaic situation, certainly—a tram stop by the Via Verdi and a dozen people waiting for transport. Just as it arrived I called out to a dark figure in front of me :

"Ciccio!"

He turned and saw me—gentle, rather short-sighted eyes behind glasses, and the smile of unforgotten friendship. Then we were swept into the tram, nudged and jostled, and there was the business of paying one's fare. I would never have chosen such a place in which to hold an important conversation, but now and again life seems to arrange things with ludicrous inappropriateness. Ducking under the elbows of strap-hangers (we are both of us small, though he a little taller than I) we managed to converge at last.

"Well, Mario! Now tell me all about yourself. What have you been doing?"

In order to make ourselves heard we had to bawl in one another's faces, such was the noise and so many were the interruptions—the constant nudging and sidling of those who wanted to get out, the arm in your face and the basket in your ribs, and the dying hiss of the doors as they closed again . . .

After our leaving the seminary our lives had for a little while run on separate but strangely parallel lines—Ciccio, under the parish church of Santa Maria degli Angeli, concerning himself with the welfare of children, and I under Materdei helping the factory workers. We then combined our efforts and joined the *Istituto Ragazzi del Popolo*—the Institute for Children of the People—a cause which seemed so splendid to us at the time, but which, alas, simply came apart in our hands owing to the utter lack of understanding, on the part of the authorities, of the problems involved. Disillusioned, we then went off in opposite directions, Ciccio attaching himself to the Oratory and I leaving Materdei for my home, from which of course I still continued my other activities.

The plans we had made together had simply collapsed, and that fact gave our unexpected meeting all the more poignancy. There was a feeling of "unfinished business". We had been frustrated, but we still had something to do, and we both knew it. This was not merely the meeting of two people who had been in a seminary together and wanted to gossip. It was a continuation, a resumption, and it had purpose.

Hubbub and klaxon horns and struggling bodies—perhaps the confusion even helped us. It is possible that in such

59

circumstances two people can isolate themselves more easily, forming a kind of protective deafness and blindness against the rest of the world.

"The *scugnizzi*, Ciccio."

"Yes, a terrible problem—terrible." He looked at me again. "You mean—but Mario, what on earth could you hope to do?"

I reminded him of my experiences with the charcoal-burners above Matese, and told him how completely convinced I was that the only way in which to reach people, to communicate with them, was to become one of them. Otherwise, how would you ever know what was in their hearts?

As the doors started to open again Ciccio looked round him in horror.

"But I should have got out ten minutes ago!"

"So should I. Never mind. But where on earth are we?"

We continued our conversation on an unfamiliar pavement.

"There's only one thing for it," I said. "I shall become a *scugnizzo* myself."

At that moment the matter became quite definite. By saying it aloud I had committed myself, and I would never draw back. I now knew and accepted the course of events.

Ciccio's face lit up at once : he knew what I meant. Then came a moment's apprehension. It would be a tough assignment. I saw him glance at my hands.

"Small," he said. "Like a boy's hands, but not like a *scugnizzo*'s hands. They'll need to be dirty. And you know that kind of dirt——"

"Of course I do. It seems to be *under* the skin. How do they manage that?"

"Just another Neapolitan trick," laughed Ciccio. "You'll have to learn it, and you'll have to learn all sorts of things. Some of them you won't like, and perhaps you won't even want to talk to me about them." He looked at me seriously. "I'm going to help you. Didn't you know?"

"Of course I did."

CHAPTER SIX

Moving Mountains

All very well, but in our enthusiasm we had both of us underestimated the difficulties. We did of course realise that to save the *scugnizzo* would not mean simply to give him food and clothes but to change his entire way of life. Not an easy task! It had been attempted by priests before (and only recently have I read of a priest who *in the sixteenth century* assumed the same responsibility). Indeed, it was a daily occurrence that priests, within their limitations, did their very best to help these urchins.

But for a priest to *become* an urchin—to dress as one and to follow to a certain extent his way of life—that was the difficulty. To anyone but us it seemed a fantastic proposition.

Everything was wrong with it; it was absurd, impossible, useless, even exhibitionistic; and yes, even scandalous too.

Moreover, as a priest you have allegiances which you cannot possibly avoid. If you are going to change your way of life as radically as that you must have official sanction for your behaviour. You can't simply follow your own inclinations, however strong they may be or however valid you think they are. You are not free to do just as you please.

It seemed to us then, as it always does to the young, that what was really wrong with the world was that it was run by people far older than ourselves, and totally incapable of understanding our point of view. How were we ever going to convince the authorities that you cannot possibly hope to reclaim and defend the *scugnizzo* if you only see him from a distance? They already knew of the tragic and appalling conditions under which these urchins were living, but they needed visual proof pushed under their eyes, if not rubbed on their noses, and I was determined that they should have it.

Fortunately a friend of mine called Salvatore was an excellent photographer, and he was obviously the right person to be roped into the venture. Although far older than I he was still young in heart and extremely responsive to any scheme that seemed progressive, humane and constructive. Moreover, he himself was well aware of the *scugnizzo* problem and horrified by it. He was only too ready to help.

And so night after night we went out together to take flashlight photographs of the conditions under which the urchins lived and slept. Useful work though it was I could not feel at all happy about it because, being still dressed as a priest, I could never seem to get close enough to it. I was remote, an alien figure, an intruder, a busybody prying into the miseries of others. I just disturbed and annoyed, I was a nuisance.

However, these photographs had to be taken and even the first—shots of conditions in the Vasto area—seemed to us almost unbelievable. You could not imagine how those ragged, dirty and homeless children, huddled together on sheets of newspaper in reeking alleys, a strange sort of coalescence of human misery, could possibly manage to survive the winter nights. And the winter nights of Naples can be more severe than most people, thinking of "the warm south", would like to suppose.

With evidence of this sort, really heartbreaking, some of it, we should surely be able to convince the authorities of the urgency of the problem. The *scugnizzo* of pre-war days was no longer the "curly-pated little rascal" exploiting his charm for the sake of survival : there was now a post-war *scugnizzo*, who was very different indeed, sullen and devious, well-versed in every vice and commercial racket ever known to civilisation : at an early age, lost as a human being. The war was over—but how long the stench of it remained!

When we had taken enough photographs to form a really impressive collection, I thought it was high time that Ciccio and I pleaded our cause.

It was a difficult and long operation, sometimes delicate and sometimes strenuous : and it involved no less than three Monsignori.

Monsignor A was so tall that he loomed over me, making me feel like an impassioned midget. He did not allow himself

Priest as vagabond

Sleepers and dogs

Sleepers and rats

The dormitory of the street

Straw for bedding

Via Forcella; home of the black market

The unloved

The *scugnizzo*'s pillow

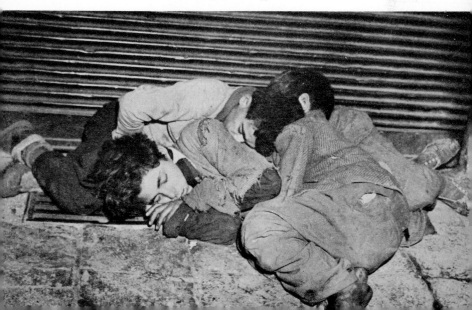

Talking to Cardinal Ascolesi

Wash and brush-up for a vagabond priest

A piece of bread and I

The Salvation Army—my turn in the queue

Some of the gang

With the gang—second from left

Now they know who I am I can walk
among them as a priest

Their first Sacrament

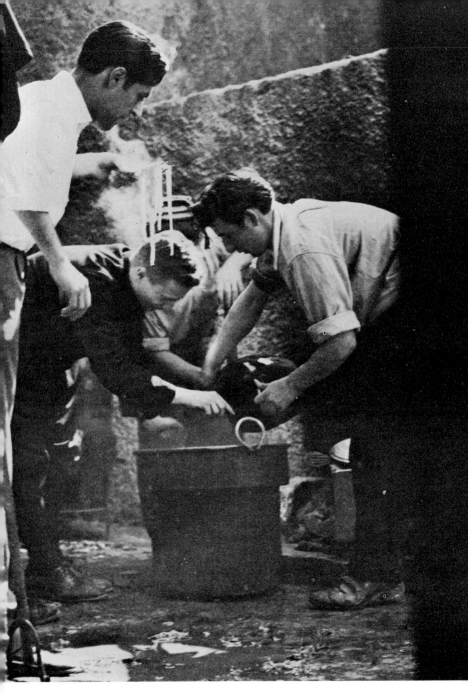

Cooking under difficulties

First days in the Casa

Bringing in the scrap-iron

A pottery class in our first school

The joy of getting a present

Talking to *scugnizzi* in my office

to seem at all impressed by what I had shown him, saying merely that he was well aware of the tragedy of these boys and could see that one could produce plenty of evidence to prove it. On the other hand he was not entirely convinced that I had the right qualifications (what should they have been, I wonder?) and doubted very much that my superiors would ever understand or consent to the idea. So as not to seem deliberately unhelpful he promised to speak to Monsignor B about it. It was perfectly clear that at this stage he did not want to get involved. A policy of non-commitment, of strict neutrality.

Home I went that day minus a few of our photographs and feeling suddenly very weary. I had pleaded our cause with, I thought, a good deal of force, and I had achieved practically nothing. It was obviously going to be necessary to move mountains.

What depressed me so much was that I felt the man had inwardly sympathised and that in reality he was not nearly as cold and indifferent as he had seemed. It was just that he was afraid—why?—to give me any definite encouragement.

Where did I go wrong? Could I have been too forceful, too impassioned? Perhaps I should try a rather more diplomatic approach. I must above all make the authorities understand that, so very far from trying to make myself into a modern saint, I was an extremely practical young man, very well aware of our everyday life and part of it : and that I would never wish to be otherwise.

And I was even now beginning to see that, to achieve my object, I might even have to use a certain amount of cunning. Yes, I had better go and see Monsignor B at once, before Monsignor A had managed to infect him with his diffidence.

Unfortunately I was too late. A had got there first, and although B was perfectly courteous—in fact even affable— he was obviously playing for safety. Assuming an expression of cautious tolerance (as though there were some sort of smell which one had not yet assessed as being nice or nasty) he listened to every word that Ciccio and I had to say. And after all that, he told us—can you believe it?—that perhaps he would need to broach the matter to a Monsignor C . . .

We found ourselves saying, almost in duet, that this third Monsignor already knew all about us and had even promised his active support.

It worked. B was at first taken aback, then visibly melted. He even went so far as to say that he would speak of the matter directly to His Eminence the Cardinal, and there was no reason why we should not have serious hopes of success.

As you can well imagine, we rushed straight for Monsignor C before B could possibly have had time for a word with him, and told him that B had already promised to interest himself in our case—indeed, that he felt perfectly certain of our being allowed to do what we wanted . . .

I confess that, in the interests of a cause in which we believed so deeply, we were deliberately playing these Monsignori off against one another. At any moment we would have them in open competition as to who would be the first to obtain the authorization of His Eminence!

And I must also confess that for diplomatic reasons I made use of an argument for which I do not really care at all. Unlike many Italians, I have no sectarian prejudices whatsoever : I respect the religions of others : because I do not agree with them, that does not mean that I automatically despise them. But I thought it prudent to point out to the Monsignori that since the war the Protestants, with considerable financial assistance from abroad, had been increasing their propaganda and that in every night in slum districts like Vasto the Salvation Army was to be found distributing hot drinks and food to the hungry *scugnizzi*. (All praise to them, I secretly thought, for who in this world without deep convictions and a sense of goodness would leave his bed on a winter's night to do such a thing?) But did not the Monsignori think that it was high time for us to learn a lesson from them? Indeed if it were not already too late? Why were we letting an entire section of society slip through our fingers, as though the Roman Catholic Church did not exist?

It was a good card to play, and they looked very thoughtful.

In a few days a clerical meeting was held, and Monsignori A, B and C introduced us formally to His Eminence the Cardinal, expounding the object of our mission with an eloquence and conviction which had so suddenly come to them.

Kneeling in front of His Eminence, Ciccio and I watched his face anxiously. As he listened his eyes kept turning from the Monsignori to us. I suppose we must have looked to him like two small children brought in for punishment, and no doubt he was wondering why there was all this fuss. His expression, puzzled at first, began to change. He looked surprised, even amazed; and then concerned. At last he smiled at us and leant forward impulsively. Putting one hand on Ciccio's shoulder and one on mine he drew us both towards him as though he suddenly wanted to embrace us.

"May Jesus bless you, my sons!" And then, in an anxious whisper: "And protect you too. *For there will be so many dangers—so many!*"

Our guardian angels A, B and C were as radiant as we were, seeming to have shed all their former reservations and nodding with satisfaction at having procured us the necessary blessing. I think they did realise in that moment that something splendid had been achieved.

As for us, we had a sudden longing for fresh air and light and the day outside. We were so jubilant that, but for our priestly clothes, we would have been capable of doing something quite mad. Boys were playing football, and I nearly joined in the game. After all, it would not have been the first time that I had played it in a soutane.

Days of planning and plotting; hours of pleading and protesting; brilliant moments of assurance and black moments of something very near to despair—these, with an almost exhausting expense of spirit, had finally given our venture the Cardinal's blessing.

It remained only to obtain the sanction of the Superior of his Oratory that my friend Ciccio should join me in becoming a *scugnizzo*, and after all we had been through, all we had achieved, it seemed a very small hurdle indeed.

But how wrong we were!

CHAPTER SEVEN

Two Hands Only

As I have already said, Ciccio had joined the community of the Oratory. I must now tell you what that means. It will not be easy to do so in measured words, but at least I can give you an impression.

This order, founded in the mid-sixteenth century, was inspired by S. Filippo, a man who had advanced and progressive ideas quite extraordinary for his time and background. It is—and this piece of information will possibly make people smile who do not quite understand the significance of it—an order which demands no vows at all, not even of chastity. S. Filippo did not consider vows necessary, since a priest, having committed and dedicated himself, should be forever far above all vows and oaths and restrictions. Why should he need some sort of certificate? This was an act of faith in priesthood, since vows, he thought, were only for the spiritually immature.

The Oratorians had once been a very flourishing community with a splendid reputation, but at the time when Ciccio joined the order it had fallen into decay, I do not know why. The Oratory itself—a vast and splendid building in Via Duomo, opposite the Cathedral of Naples—was in fact inhabited only by Ciccio, his Superior, and one other priest! It scarcely seems possible that this echoing palace, capable of housing whole regiments, should at that time have contained only three people. And in the very middle of Naples. How can they have borne the emptiness?

Let me describe the place. Through a tall doorway you walk into a tiled courtyard begun in 1586, in the middle of which is a beautiful marble-faced well with scrolled ironwork like the tendrils of vines. Around it there are vaulted cloisters with grey marble columns. The colours throughout the place are white, grey and a warm coral, and even though the architecture wanders smoothly on through centuries—as so often happens in Italy, and as is indeed inevitable when a building is so vast in conception that it takes years upon years to construct—these colours seem to persist and to give to beautifully proportioned doorways and windows, and to lofty diminishing corridors, a feeling of unity. Another virtue that the Oratory has in its architecture is the power to confront you, in the midst of a cold whitewashed simplicity, with something rich and ornate—

perhaps a towering sixteenth-century doorway—that takes your breath away.

There is a second courtyard, noble in proportion, in which flourishing lemon trees may feed on the remains of bygone Oratorian priests buried in the crypt beneath. On the first floor of this quadrangle alone there are forty rooms at least—and there are floors above and below! Indeed, nobody seems to know how many rooms there are in the Oratory, and I am convinced that if you tried to count them you could begin all over again and reach a different total. Finally let me say that there is a huge and very important library, a picture-gallery and a museum of ancient vestments, and of course a large church and also a chapel of which you will hear more later.

Forgive this short conducted tour, but it really has point and poignancy, as in the context you will have gathered.

All this. And three people in it.

Out in the streets there were kids of seven or eight years old with nowhere to sleep, hundreds of them in the rain and wind, fighting for the privilege of lying by the grating of a baker's shop that would give them a little warmth, kids for whom one sheet of newspaper was as good as a blanket, and their only pillow another lad's ribs.

It was horrible. The gap, the disparity—impossible to bear. It made nonsense of civilisation itself and Ciccio was tormented. Just imagine, with the problem of the *scugnizzi* so much in your mind, walking down those empty corridors.

He and I had of course discussed so many times the wonderful opportunities that the enormous Oratory suggested, and with the presumption of young enthusiasm had mentally re-arranged the entire place to suit our own purposes. Dormitories and school-rooms here—and there the workshops in which *scugnizzi* would be taught trades—and then, of course, kitchens and refectories—oh, we were quite ready to start! Permission from the Father Provost was all that was needed.

All that was needed.

A telephone rang and I picked up the receiver eagerly, knowing that I would hear Ciccio.

"You spoke to him?"

"Yes, Mario."

Only two words, but somehow his voice told me that everything had gone wrong.

"But what did he *say*?"

"I'm sorry. We shall have to begin all over again."

"No, Ciccio, listen—I'm asking you what *he* said—the Father Provost. If he's refused—well, why? Oh, it doesn't seem possible—all those empty rooms—!"

"Well, I suppose it may have been for a mixture of reasons."

"Such as what?"

There was a pause and I could hear Ciccio sigh deeply. He had been demolished by the interview, and of course it would take him a little time to become rational about it.

"Oh, for one thing he may have wanted peace and quiet in the place."

"Nonsense. You could let all hell loose in one corner of it, and have all the *scugnizzi* in Naples run screeching down a corridor, and nobody would hear a sound."

"Yes, I agree, Mario—but you see—oh, I'm not upholding his point of view—it *is* a place that has been sacrosanct for centuries."

"He should have given you a better reason than that."

"There was probably a personal one too . . . afraid that I'd get too involved in the scheme, too absorbed? And that I'd leave his community?"

It would have been unkind to say to Ciccio that three minus one equals two. In any case I had a tremendous respect even then for the Oratorian order, and the fact that it was momentarily in decay had really nothing to do with the point.

"And there's another thing," Ciccio was saying. "We hadn't told him about all this in the beginning. I suppose it hurt his feelings."

His feelings. Really, had one to discuss the delicate susceptibilities of people while the problem of the children of Naples became an international scandal? For the moment I felt quite sick, and the telephone itself, the coin box and the stand underneath it, seemed suddenly to have become a grizzled elderly person through whose mouth Ciccio was no longer speaking. This was the voice of Authority saying forever, "*No! No, you can't. No, it isn't possible. No, it could never be permitted. No, it would be wrong. No, we couldn't allow it. No, no, no, and NO!*"

"Mario, are you still there?"

"Yes, Ciccio—I'm sorry. I was just thinking."

"Well?"

"We can't possibly go through all this again."

"You sound so unhappy, Mario—"

"I'm not unhappy, I'm angry. And I'm more than angry, I'm perfectly furious. Do something, will you?"

"But what more can I do?"

"You can arrange an appointment with your Father Provost!"

"To see whom?"

"Me, dear Ciccio."

*   *   *   *

The meeting was arranged, and I went to the Oratory. It was one of those bitter days of late December in which old stones, so hot to touch in August and September, give out a sort of long-inherited cold that contrives to combine dampness with a feeling of vague despair. Especially when you find yourself in a sixteenth century building of the kind that never knows heat unless it gets burnt to the ground.

We met in the Cappella dell'Assunta, opposite the side entrance to the large church of the Oratory. This beautiful chapel itself would have seemed to many to be a sizeable church—barrel-roofed and elaborately frescoed. Figures of saints lean out from the walls, and the heavens above you are almost over-populated. There is superb gilding on the altar and also on the gallery, where there stands a small and very ancient church organ that I must one day try to play.

Nowadays this chapel has become a sort of dump for vague ecclesiastical objects, most of them dusty and some good and some bad, pictures, gilt carvings, the bric-à-brac

of centuries; but at that time, when I came to see Ciccio's
Father Provost, the chapel was clear—cold and clear—and
by the altar the Provost, not in his priestly vestments but in
a pair of ordinary slacks held up by cross-over braces, was
trying to reconstruct the crumbling remnants of an old
Christmas Crib, tottering camels and Wise Men without
foundations and a collapsing manger. Beside him there was
a pot of glue, and it was obviously very necessary.

I could have used it myself. In my impatience I was
longing to glue this fidgeting Provost firmly into a spot
where I could talk and talk to him without his being able
to escape.

Every word seemed to imply a negative. And every word
seemed to take so long to utter.

He did not consider that the work we proposed doing
would be useful, productive or necessary.

"But, with all respect, is it wrong to want to help the
scugnizzi?"

"Not wrong, no. The desire to do so is of course admir-
able. But are you really asking me to allow a member of my
community"—he spoke as though it consisted of hundreds
—"to expose himself to the dangers of the streets?"

"You mean—you think he would be contaminated?"

"Of course. How could it be otherwise if he associated
with people of evil life?"

The crossed braces, the smell of fish glue and the one
guttering candle—they were all driving me mad. I could
not look at Ciccio. For his sake, above all, I must speak with
patience and respect. If I exploded, it would be he who
suffered. And the voice went on and on—pausing now and

75

again as a wooden shepherd was found to be in need of repair.

"There is another thing too . . . these people . . . these *scugnizzi* . . . I am told that they use knives. Even razors. Now, how would you two propose . . . to defend yourselves? And, indeed, how would you justify your actions in doing so?"

One could go on like this for ever and reach no conclusion. I said as quietly as I could:

"You know, Father, that His Eminence has already given us his sanction and his blessing?"

"So I am told. It was splendid of him, and for you a very great privilege . . . but of course, as Don Spada's Superior . . . I am entitled to a written copy of this permit, so that I can appeal to Rome . . . before making my final decision."

I was dazed. With how much agony had that *spoken* assent been obtained! And now we were being asked for written evidence.

Priestly caution and diffidence were by no means unknown to me. Even in my brief experience I had encountered many inexplicable delays and soft excuses: on one occasion even a Prior's afternoon nap, not to be interrupted on any account, had prevented me from carrying out my duties. Sometimes I had even begun to feel that I was in a pale blue vacuum which nothing must ever be allowed to disturb.

But I have a temper, and I could bear this no longer. Regardless of Ciccio's feelings, or of the Provost's, I shouted into the beautiful Cappella dell'Assunta, · taking full advantage of its perfectly splendid acoustics:

"Very well, then—I shall go out into the streets *alone*! And as a *scugnizzo*! And God help me!"

Gluepot, candle, braces—I rushed away from them all, through the paved courtyard and the tall doors and out into the crowded Via Duomo.

From now on I was to be alone.

And I confess that I was afraid.

CHAPTER EIGHT

Urchin
without
Knife

Yes, afraid of beginning alone.

Even for a layman it is not easy to wear unfamiliar clothes, to walk in a different way, to adopt other habits, to plunge suddenly into a world in which the customs, the mentality and the speech are all quite different from what he is used to. You can imagine how much more difficult it is for a priest, for whom the black soutane is a symbol of his whole way of life. To put it aside seems at first like an act of betrayal. Something is fundamentally wrong. He is more than uneasy, he is lost.

In spite of my outburst of anger I did not storm my way into the *scugnizzo's* world without some degree of preparation. It would have been silly to do so without any clear idea of what I would be able to do for them when I had won their confidence.

A certain amount of plotting and planning was necessary. On impulse I went back to the parish church of Materdei and asked for help from the confraternity. After some deliberation they were good enough to offer me a small subsidiary church (S. Gennaro a Materdei) which I myself, with a few helping hands, had some while ago rescued from utter collapse in order to find premises for a youth club. This they had totally forgotten, and made me a present of what was in effect my own piece of work. Still, it was something, and suppressing a smile I told them how grateful I was for their material help.

Human help was by no means so easy to find. I had met many young and energetic priests, men of enterprise and imagination, high-spirited and unconventional, and you would have thought that among them there would be at least one who would be glad to join with me in rescuing the *scugnizzi*. But no, their assistance was limited to brotherly counsel, and though they were all dedicated to self-sacrifice not one of them would have dreamed of sharing with me the hazards of the pavement—insomnia, vermin, dirt and cold.

So often I thought of my friend Ciccio, the little priest who would most willingly, if only he were allowed, have put away his soutane and followed me; but technicalities and Crossed Braces had separated us.

With considerable subterfuge he and I did manage to meet now and again and had even contrived to make contact with several *scugnizzi*, which was at least a beginning. I remember that one of these poor wretches was called O Zelluso (The Mangy One) who had lost all his hair through ringworm. Even his companions, who were by no means squeamish, were disgusted by him. A greasy old cap had stuck to the scabs and seemed to be part of his head. To remove the cap and to attack his cranium with penicillin ointment (which, alas, did nothing) was a performance which Ciccio managed without flinching. Separately and together we managed to acquire a number of *scugnizzi*, and in the end—as a Christmas treat—Ciccio organised a supper for them.

And—believe it or not—with the support and blessing of his Superior! (Let me now atone for anything I have said about Crossed Braces. He is a profoundly good man, and I have ended by joining his order. The trouble at this period was simply that he was not yet ready to accept the revolutionary idea of a priest becoming a *scugnizzo*.)

As for the supper, I was of course mad with jealousy. I would have loved to have been there, to have helped, to have organised, but I did not dare to put in an appearance. Having lost my temper so noisily in the Cappella dell' Assunta I had to keep away from it.

Ciccio was in his own quiet fashion making the best of things, and achieving, or so it seemed to me at the moment, more than I. But there were so many things to be done, and I could no longer put off the moment in which I turned into a *scugnizzo* myself.

"When is it to be?"

"Tomorrow."

"Good." A hand on my shoulder. "Mind if I come with you?"

The hand was not that of a priest. No, it was Salvatore's —the hand of a hard-working middle-aged photographer who spent most of his days developing negatives in a dark room and was now proposing to walk into the greater blackness of a Neapolitan night with me and bring out of it whatever horrors there were.

"Salvatore, you with so much to do—! Later, yes—if you will. In fact I can see now that I'm going to need your help."

"What time tomorrow?"

I smiled. Such goodness is never to be pushed aside. We made our appointment.

*   *   *   *

It always seems to me wrong for priests to discuss clerical matters with their families, whose advice, since they are not of the church, is bound to be of worldly and selfish nature. They cannot be expected to understand one's point of view and should never be asked to do so.

On the other hand, I could not possibly disappear from my mother's house night after night without a word of explanation. She had to be told why, in bitter January weather, I was exchanging my comfortable bed for a wet pavement, and my cassock for rags.

The result was, of course, an extremely painful scene. She knew about my helping the poor community of charcoal-burners above Matese, and understood why I could not have gone to them dressed as a priest. But this new scheme of mine seemed to her altogether different and she listened to me with growing horror.

"Oh no, Mario, you can't! I shall be terrified for you, every moment of the night. And just listen to the wind! Haven't you seen the bonfires in the streets? It's *freezing*, Mario—"

She burst into tears and I did not know what to do to comfort her. Embarrassed, I could only stand there caressing her face and her hair while she clung to me.

"I must go."

"Don't leave me, Mario."

"I've got to meet somebody." I disengaged myself as gently as I could. "It may help you to know that I shan't be alone."

"But *I* shall."

Then she made one more effort to pull me back to her and I could not bear it any longer. I escaped and ran down the stairs, leaving her sobbing distractedly.

Salvatore would be waiting for me in his studio and I was already late. Fortunately he had only just managed to get rid of the last of his relatives—they did not care for the scheme either and were trying to talk him out of it.

"Let's get going," said Salvatore. "I've got your clothes." He picked up the bundle of rags and put it under his arm.

*   *   *   *

I must explain that I had chosen the cell of a Dominican friend of mine as my changing room—at the beginning of this book I described the priest who went into it (snatching at a cigarette butt on the way) and the vagabond who came out. The reason for my choice of this monastery was that it is in a dark and narrow lane, and it seemed to me sensible to find a quiet and inconspicuous spot for the transformation.

My trousers were an old pair of Salvatore's, worn and stained with the chemicals he used for his work, and the shirt looked as though it could have come out of a dustbin. As for the shoes, they were of different sizes—a subtle touch perhaps, but one that I did not appreciate at first, when I started to move about. And they were of course laced with string. Then that greasy old cap, and finally, as a small concession to the fact that we were in the depths of winter, a faded and threadbare scarf. Oddly enough, this seemed the most ruffianly garment of the lot, especially in combination with my stubbly chin—for of course I had stopped shaving for several days.

This Dominican friend gave us hot food and an encouraging glass of wine, and after a few moments' conversation both he and the good Salvatore were completely silent while I changed, knowing that for me it was a moment of great significance.

It is not easy to be explicit about what I felt . . . Yes, as I say, it is an odd thing for a priest to put off his soutane, which as a visible declaration of his way of life becomes part of him. And yet when I did so, I did not feel in the least like a layman, for so strong was my belief in the rightness of what I was doing that I could have been putting on even another kind of habit, ragged though it was. These indeed were the vestments of the poor and the hungry and the small and the homeless and loveless; and these I had to wear in order to join their number and begin to understand them.

Other sensations came to me as we began to walk down the street, the first being that I was walking in a completely different fashion (and no wonder, with odd shoes) and also that I was possibly overplaying my part. It would be so easy, with such an abrupt change, to give a very amateur performance which would be credible to nobody, and least of all to the *scugnizzi*—whom above all I had to convince. I was not yet sure that the pavements themselves would teach me : as of course they did in the end. But in the meantime I felt I was merely an impostor.

I was also aware that this operation was none too easy for Salvatore himself. Not that he ever dresses in the height of fashion; his clothes are always plain and serviceable; but in comparison with me he looked like the smartest man in Naples, and I could not help reflecting that if he ran into friends of his they might well wonder what on earth he was doing in such very dubious company.

And it happened. At two o'clock in the morning in the Piazza Plebiscito. And, even worse—they were *mutual* friends of ours.

They stopped to greet Salvatore and I shuffled on, convinced that they had seen through me and knew who I was and that some appalling scandal was imminent. I was making for the church of S. Francesco di Paola, where I knew he would come to find me. Hours seemed to pass before he arrived.

"Salvatore, *what did they say?*"

He smiled.

"Now, what are you worried about?"

"But they must have known me, I've talked to them so many times!"

"Mario, they had absolutely no idea who you were."

For the moment that seemed impossible.

"Are you *sure*?"

I need not have questioned him. Salvatore is a fine person. His mouth has humour and strength and his eyes have complete honesty. He can be forceful and direct in speech, and you can take a mere gesture of his as a firm statement.

"Why don't you offer me a seat?" said Salvatore. "These stones are yours now, you know."

We laughed and sat down on the steps.

I must explain.

The Piazza Plebiscito is one of the largest and finest in Naples, and it can swallow an entire bus-centre without losing its architectural integrity. On one side is the Royal Palace—rows of well-proportioned windows, and on either side of the main entrance two rather silly brick sentry boxes asking for toy soldiers. The colours on this side of the building are gold and white and one can look at it with pleasure.

Opposite, where Salvatore and I were sitting, is the very impressive and lovely church of S. Francesco di Paola. From the great dome there stretches a semicircular colonnade like an embrace of two arms. Here the colours are flaming coral and grey, very lovely together.

We did not of course come here for aesthetic reasons. I mention colours and proportions only so that you should see where we were, that first night. There are, in fact, far more significant things to say about the place.

First, we have an old Neapolitan song:

> *"He who has no home*
> *Has still S. Francesco di Paola . . . "*

Which means of course that, somewhat like the crypt of St. Martin's-in-the-Fields in London, this wide portico is a place for down-and-outs. A number of *scugnizzi*, but not so much the little ones. Their elders frequent the place even in the daytime, and you may find them at any hour playing among the columns, especially if one of them has managed to acquire a football.

And here we were, yawning among the recumbent bodies in the early hours of the morning. I laughed suddenly.

"The palace opposite, Salvatore—that's where I go for the Holy Year Committee and where the sentry is so correct and formal. He always salutes me and stamps his heels."

"And if he could see you now?"

"Exactly. It'd be a boot on my backside."

"Well—if you'll excuse the phrase, I think I'll go to bed."

"I too."

Marble was cold marble, but it was luxury compared with what I slept on later, stones and mud and newspaper in back alleys.

The homeless were lying in various positions, some straight out and the head twisted to one side as though not wanting to hear something painful; some making pillows of one another, and some in the simple foetal position of a child in the womb; that was most painful of all, for they had still to be born. Into what?

Into a life that I had to try to make for them.

I scarcely remember if I slept that night, but in any case it is difficult to talk of sleep, as we know it, under those conditions. There are so many kinds of "sleep"—from an uneasy dozing in which one is aware of every movement of neighbours or the rustle of a rat in the garbage, to an exhaustion so profound that you can hardly raise yourself from the stones, having not only slept on them but sculptured your body to their shape, learning only too well their coldness and dampness and unkindness. And there are also the uneasy hours of the vermin-ridden.

That first night was only a rehearsal.

Promptly at eight o'clock the next morning I was at the Liceo Sannazzaro, where classes larger than they should ever be were waiting for me to teach them.

I did so for five hours, then fell asleep on my desk.

But that would never do, for a job like this demanded toughness and I was determined to acquire it.

CHAPTER NINE

The City
Wakes
at Night

Five thousand five hundred tourists came streaming ashore from ships in port, looking for a night's entertainment; some for innocent diversion, some for less reputable reasons, and others in complete ignorance of what might happen to them if they fell in with the unscrupulous. In no time at all every one of them seemed to be surrounded by touts and ponces and petty thieves.

Where do such people come from? The world is suddenly full of them, though in the daytime they do not seem to exist. They come out of the stones and out of antiquity, owning nothing. Some of them do not even own their own bodies. This darkness is their day, and it became my day too. Small as many a *scugnizzo*, sharp-eyed, shuffling in unmatched shoes and stooping suddenly for a cigarette-butt, I joined them. And I confess I was fascinated by what I saw and heard.

Even those people who have also a daytime existence, and are familiar to you, seem to acquire a different personality at night. The cab-driver is no longer a kerbside fatalist waiting for his fare to arrive : he must importune feverishly while there are still people about, and his brain is full of profitable information—telephone numbers of call-girls, addresses of houses of assignation and doubtful hotels, closing times of cinemas and night-clubs, arrivals of Liberty Boats from the American Navy. His whole nature seems to change. Mild-tempered as he may be by day, he will even find himself defending his rights with his fists. (I have seen many a fight between cab-drivers, and one that I shall never forget. A lame driver on crutches was knocked down by a sturdy rival and fell squirming helplessly in the Via Caracciolo, like an octopus on dry land.)

The beggar under the stars, too, is different from the beggar by day; quieter and calmer, less aggressive, for at this time he has his regular patrons and knows that he does not need to exert himself. The late-opening shopkeeper changes too : instead of flattering and cajoling his clients he even manages to give the impression that he is bestowing a favour on them.

In short, the night dispenses with ceremony. Humanity is less conventional and more primitive, and—I cannot help saying it—more sincere. There are few pretences. The masks are gone. We can sense our roots. I could not help feeling, when I began to prowl at night, that I too was far nearer to my own self.

It was a kind of release, a feeling of lightness, ease and self-confidence. My rags were a passport to the most ill-famed and dangerous alleys—or dangerous they would have seemed. But danger had gone, since I had nothing to gain or lose.

*   *   *   *

In these nights I had less need of Salvatore's company, and there were times when I even forgot his existence; so absorbed was I by this new world that I was like a child who had just managed to walk and was beginning to discover the nature of things. I was busy learning the lessons of the pavement. I talked to everybody and began to know my way about. But I was still alone.

It was time, obviously, to join a gang.

I knew that the slums of the Vasto district were the haunts of many scugnizzi, who between eleven o'clock and midnight would arrive in numbers to benefit from the hot milk, bread and chocolate distributed by the Salvation Army. Oh, how I would have liked to thank these good Protestant friends whose existence I had used as an argument to plead my own cause! They had in fact helped me to gain the Cardinal's blessing. And now they provided me with the perfect setting, the exact battleground, that I really needed. If I asked bread and milk of them they would accept me without question. And I would meet scugnizzi from every part of Naples.

One night I left the Dominican monastery in rags even more wretched, but with face and hands that I realised were still far too white. I had done my best to smear them, but never did I manage to achieve that oddly subcutaneous dirt that is characteristic of the long-unscrubbed *scugnizzo*. I was of course unshaven. (And I cannot tell you how painful it was for me, who am bodily fastidious, to face my mixed classes at school every morning with several days' growth of beard.)

On the way to the Vasto district something happened which gave me courage. In the narrow lane of San Pietro a Maiella I came across the skulking figure of a lad who, startled by my sudden appearance, seemed at first to be wondering if he had not better bolt for the crowded street beyond, for if I had attacked him here nobody would have known anything about it. But he stood his ground, and as I came up to him he asked me for a light. I saw then that the hand holding the cigarette-butt was trembling.

He was frightened of me.

*　　　*　　　*　　　*

Now here they were, over thirty *scugnizzi* seething near the Via Firenze, and an even larger number squatting round the grating of a baker's oven. (Bless the bakers of Naples: the warmth of their pavement gratings comforts the homeless and may have saved many a child from pneumonia: but I must say that the smell of their fresh baking, one of the sweetest smells on earth, can be a torture to empty stomachs.)

I pulled out of my pocket a fag-end, rank and juicy, re-flecting that I would now be forced to smoke these instead of my usual cigarettes. And then I joined the group by the baker's grating, squatting down beside them without a word and as though I had a perfect right to be there. Had I fal-tered then it would have been fatal, and there would have been no story to write.

It is time to explain that the *scugnizzi* organise themselves in bands of six to about twenty. They have a "leader" who has usually imposed his will on them by jungle methods. He is an accomplished pilferer himself and an organiser of thefts by others, ruling them all by being able to punch or kick a little harder. He is skilful in avoiding the police and can give warning of their arrival almost by instinct. Moreover he has made and maintained useful contacts in dubious circles and has influence. He knows what is going on. He knows what can be done. He is not merely in command, he is indispensable.

However, there is a certain elasticity in numbers, for some leave one gang to join another; and more arrive to take their place. Naturally there are always unstable ele-ments, for there are constant rumours that one gang does better than its rival.

There is a certain separateness too, in spite of the gang-mentality, for each member is perfectly capable of cheating one of his fellows without compunction. Should he fall asleep in an unguarded moment, should he show weakness or hesi-tation, one or even a conspiracy of his companions will con-trive to rob him of the little that he has. If you are a *scug-nizzo* you are without mercy, even for your own kind.

But to return to the leader: he is of course older than the rest—between sixteen and twenty—and the youngest are victims of his system of exploitation. They are usually sent out on scrounging expeditions, begging the "left-overs" from restaurants, hotels, barracks and convents, or even articles of clothing from private houses. Being small and miserable they excite more pity.

Many were their devices for earning money, but one of the strangest and most original I ever encountered was the "gimmick" known as *posteggia*.

A boy is suddenly taken ill. He groans, writhes, claps his hands to his stomach and falls down on the pavement. Moreover, he even foams at his mouth. It is a convincing performance, and a most pathetic one. His anxious companions call the attention of everybody in sight to this agonising spectacle, and the money comes down like snow in winter.

In the gang I finally joined there was an expert at the game and the secret of it was ten *lire*'s worth of citrate of magnesium, swallowed a few minutes before the performance. It never failed to work. Foam from the mouth, like detergent issuing from a drain, covered everything, and compassionate onlookers thrust their hands in their pockets for alms. An epileptic, poor lad! When the effect wore off and recovery was inevitable, you took up the money and ran—to divide it and quarrel over it round the corner.

For the little ones there were other tasks too: they must contribute to the gang a percentage of the tobacco they have managed to pick up; and also, being the lightest in weight, they must form the apex of the pyramid in "snow-gathering" —stealing laundry from the lines strung over back alleys.

And even sexually they were exploited with brutality.

*   *   *   *

Somehow the Vasto district had become the centre of gravity for all the *scugnizzi* of Naples. Naturally there must be the ringleader of all ringleaders, and that night he was a tough little creature called O Chiattone (Fatty).

I had started on another fag-end even nastier than the first when he strolled up to me. I was sitting, and the tip of my cap was on a level with his thighs. He rapped me on the head.

"Who are you?"

(I had already asked myself the same question, looking in the glass before I left the monastery.)

"Come on, now," he said. "Who *are* you?"

He jerked the peak of my cap. I stood up at once, knowing instinctively what I must do, realising that to make peace with this creature I must make war on him first. I stared at him aggressively. And then I spat in his face.

"That's who I am!"

I could feel through the back of my head that this incident had excited the whole gang. There was a silence, a concentration of interest. I had to follow this up, for I was playing not only to the ringleader but to his own public. I stuffed my left hand into my pocket, and with my right hand I caught him by the arm.

"What's the matter with you?" I demanded. "I've got a right to a bit of warmth, haven't I, same as anyone else? And something to eat too, and who's stopping me?"

O Chiattone took it. My anger had surprised him (and the weak and vulnerable can, when roused, give far more show of violence than the strong.)

He gave a sour grin and pulled out of his pocket a razor blade. He looked at it, hesitated, then handed it to me.

"I'd have carved you," he said. "I'd have carved you so your own mother wouldn't have known you. But you got your hand in your pocket before I did. So here you are."

Still looking at him I took the razor blade abruptly. This was somehow a rite, a solemn ceremony of which the passers-by were completely unaware. It may sound easy in the telling, but it was none too easy to achieve.

Anyhow, I was accepted. I was now—and officially—a *scugnizzo*.

CHAPTER TEN

Food from
the Hands
of Strangers

It will help you to visualize my companions if I tell you
their names, for names bestowed by the pavement are always
descriptive. As time went on I heard them with monotonous
frequency.

Apart from O Chiattone (Fatty), the leader of the whole
rabble, there was O Zelluso (Mangy) whom you have also
met in a previous chapter. Another was called Totò (after
the comedian) and there were also Suricillo (Little Mouse),
Tarzan (The Strong One), Portaerei (Aircraft Carrier),
Zucculella (Drain Rat), O Cinese (Chink-eyes), O Barbuso
(Whiskers), O Muzzo (One-armed), O Zuoppo (Lame
Duck), Cap' 'e Provola (Cheese-head, or Stupid), Cap' 'e

mbomma (Big Head), Cap' 'e lignamme (Wooden Head), and Perocchio (Louse). And when Salvatore finally came on the scene, many days later, he too joined the ranks of the anonymous and was known as O Maresciallo (Quartermaster) because of his rather peremptory way of speaking.

If he had been with me when I first joined the gang his presence would have been an embarrassment. It was essential for me to act independently, sensing the mood of the *scugnizzi* and the colour of any situation, living my life by momentary instinct and inspiration, without advice or admonition. All night I would spend with these creatures, vanishing during the day to fulfil my engagements and obligations which, as time went on, began to weigh on me rather heavily. I was doing far too many things and felt sometimes that I was doing none of them well, because I was so tired. Nodding in class, nodding on the Holy Year Committee—and then there was the diocesan centre where I was Vice-assistant, helping the workers . . . No, it was all too much, and although I wanted to be four people in one it was not physically possible. Something had to go and I decided to leave the diocesan centre which absorbed so much of my time. For the moment at least one burden had to be lifted.

What did the gang think of my daily disappearances? They asked no questions but I am almost sure that they thought I was "working" the trams and trolleybuses as a pickpocket. It would have been a likely assumption and such activities were regarded as highly creditable. Later on I actually found myself taking part, though a very minor one, in a wallet-stealing episode in a tram.

But as for Salvatore—O Maresciallo!—I found I had to appeal for his help once again. I needed more photographs of the face of night, having seen what I had seen.

Not only did I need them as incontrovertible evidence to put before the world, but I realised that I would need them also for the *scugnizzi* themselves, when the moment was ripe for me to reveal myself to them as a priest, so that they would be able to recognise me as being one of their number. I had to be identifiable, or my plan would not work.

I must be honest too and confess that in insisting on more photographs there may have been a touch of vanity on my part—not, I hope, the exhibitionism of which I had been warned!—but it did seem to me that I was doing something really constructive and worthwhile and that it should not go unrecorded.

And so back came Salvatore with his camera and his flash-bulbs to photograph the unloved and the homeless lying in corners, on straw, on newspaper, pillowed on one another, sharing the street with dogs and even rats. The quickness of the flash did not disturb them at all, but it disturbed the police considerably : at the corner of an alley they would see a flare of light and come racing after us. *Photographs of the slums of Naples must never be published! Tourists might see them!*

Often we had to take to our heels, Salvatore in one direction and I in another, and then waste the rest of the night in trying to find one another since we had had no chance to plan our rendezvous. I cannot think how many times we must have chased each other round the alleys.

As for photographs that included me, it was of course

quite impossible to take them in full view of the gang and without any explanation or excuse. The obvious solution was to photograph the Salvation Army at work, for all of us came to take bread and milk from their hands and I would be among them, waiting my turn.

Salvatore did wonders. His abrupt but humorous way of speaking won him friends on all sides. He gave cigarettes to the *scugnizzi* (a gesture unfailingly popular) and also managed to make friends with the Salvation Army, who seemed to be grateful for his cordiality and understanding.

They were only too aware of the quite considerable hostility that surrounded them. It is one thing to leave your warm bed in the middle of the night to give food and drink to the hungry and thirsty, but quite another matter to be praised for doing so.

"Why should Protestants, of all people, behave like this? What are they up to? Is this some form of insidious propaganda? Do they really think that they can buy our allegiance with their milk and their bread? We will take anything that they have to offer, naturally, but we are not fools!"

Personally, I have no sectarian feelings whatsoever. For me a good man is a good man and that is the end of the matter. When I took my place in the Salvation Army queue it was with gratitude and respect, even with a certain envy since in a way they had stolen a march on me. All praise to them, since they had provided a palliative.

But the roots of the evil had still to be pulled up.

*   *   *   *

"Listen, Salvatore—please go off and have a glass of wine or a cup of coffee or something. You're exhausted, don't fight it any longer."

"Well, I *am* a bit dry. What time is it?"

"I don't wear a watch."

"Oh no, of course not. It's—I can't believe it—it's after half past five! But we can still get something to drink somewhere."

"I can't."

"Why, Mario?"

"Because very soon I have to say Mass."

"I'm sorry. I'd forgotten. Well, let's cut it out."

"Don't cut it out at all. You go off and get what you can. Leave me."

"How can I leave you when you're thirsty too?"

"Please leave me, Salvatore. I mean that."

"Oh well . . . goodnight, then. *Ciao*!"

"*Ciao*, Salvatore."

* * * *

And the next evening he would be back with his cigarettes for the *scugnizzi* and the Salvation Army, winking covertly at me and making friends in both camps.

Then an absurd thing happened.

It happened at a time when I had varied my disguise a little—another old cap and an even more disreputable muffler. Then along came Salvatore to photograph us all taking food from the Salvation Army, and this time he had brought a friend with him, a young engineer, whose function it was to control the "crowd scenes"—in fact to group us all into a shape that was photographically possible.

I tried hard to make my appearance in the middle of these proceedings, but Salvatore's friend kept pushing me into the background. Only after many shots did I manage to get into the picture.

Later, I went to Salvatore's studio and was greeted with black looks.

"Oh, so you've shown up at last. I must say, it's kind of you."

"What d'you mean, Salvatore?"

He turned on me with furious eyes and an indignant spread of hands.

"Listen. What am I doing? Am I a fool?"

"But, Salvatore—"

"Please. Am I a married man?"

"Yes, you're married."

"And have I a family?"

"Of course, yes. You've a family."

"Very well, then, I'm a married man and I have a family, and I am never never at home, not even at night. That's a fine thing! And all because of you and your *scugnizzi*."

"Salvatore, please don't speak to me like this!"

"How can I help it? I'm tired, I'm thirsty, I've no life at all, and what does that matter to you? I come to the Vasto district to take photographs of you with the Salvation Army, and you can't even be bothered to turn up. Are you trying to make a monkey of me?"

"But you're wrong—"

"Oh no, I'm not taking it any longer. I'm finished."

"You're wrong, Salvatore, I was *there*! Have you developed the negatives?"

"Yes."

"Then please let me see them."

He seemed to be gone for a long time and I was unhappy. Then he came back with his hands full. I took the negatives from him and held them up to the light.

"No, I'm not there . . . nor there . . . that friend of yours kept pushing me away—"

"Oh Mario"—Salvatore's voice dropped a whole octave —"don't tell me you were that blasted *scugnizzo* who insisted on trying to steal the picture?"

"Probably. Yes—look!—there I am."

Salvatore looked at the negative with and without his glasses. Then he said:

"My dear friend, I didn't even recognise you."

*   *   *   *

Then one night Salvatore had a dangerous rival. At about 10.30 a stranger to the Vasto district was asking about the *"Signorine"*, as the Salvation Army lasses were called (their leader was always referred to as The Porter on account of his peaked cap, so familiar at the entrances to blocks of offices). Would they be coming here tonight, and would they be distributing food?

I recognised this man perfectly well, though he could not possibly identify me. He was a journalist-photographer from *Il Giornale*, and only recently he had called on me in the

office of the Holy Year Committee to ask if he could board
the first of the pilgrim steamers with his camera. On that
occasion I had done my best to help him, and it was extremely fortunate that he was to some extent in my debt.

He was told to come back between eleven and midnight,
and when he reappeared he was clasping the camera and
flash-bulb case to his bosom as though convinced that they
would be stolen from him in the first five minutes. As soon
as the Salvation Army arrived he took his photographs with
feverish haste, thanked everybody with a rather nervous
smile and walked off through the Vasto labyrinth in the
direction of the station, relieved that he had not had his
throat cut.

But he did not like it at all that I was following him. He
heard my footsteps and could feel my presence through the
back of his head. One brief frightened glance over his
shoulder, as though to convince himself that he had not lost
his way, and he quickened his pace considerably. I quickened
mine and could almost imagine the hair rising on his head.
This was an absurd nocturnal marathon, but it was essential
for me to speak to him out of earshot of my companions.

When we reached the large busy piazza in front of the
station, where I knew he would feel a little more at ease, I
called him by name and he wheeled round in astonishment.

"You *know* me?"

I assumed a polished Tuscan accent that made nonsense
of my uncouth appearance.

"But of course I do. Don't you remember that we've met
before?"

Never have I seen anyone look more confused.

"I'm sorry, I—no, I really don't remember."

"A few days ago you came to the Royal Palace, to the office of the Holy Year Committee. It was I who got you permission to photograph the pilgrims."

"I saw a priest—"

"You saw Don Borrelli. And I am Don Borrelli."

"No!"

Confused before, he now looked like a man who could never again believe anything he saw or heard. It happened that I was standing directly under a street-lamp, and I smiled and pulled off my cap.

"Excuse the beard."

Recognition dawned and he held out his hand. And then he burst out laughing with relief and pleasure. Or could there have been a touch of anger at having been tricked into thinking me a *scugnizzo*? At all events we laughed together and I was accepted.

"But *why*, Father—?"

I explained my work to him very briefly and he understood the point at once.

"Please realise," I told him, "that if you publish those photographs in tomorrow's paper you'll simply ruin all that I'm trying to do. It's too early. I've got a long way to go yet before I can establish myself as a *scugnizzo* and a priest at the same time."

"Oh dear . . . And it was so difficult to take them, because you know what the police attitude is."

"Indeed I do."

"Anyway, what you're doing really ought to be documented."

"I'm seeing to that. But I beg of you to leave it in my hands. It's for me to judge the right moment."

"Then what d'you want me to do?"

"Let me have those negatives—I'm perfectly prepared to pay for them. Give me them tomorrow."

His eyes looked troubled and his mind seemed to have transferred itself to a distant office building.

"I don't know what the Sub-editor is going to say. It was he who gave me this assignment." Then his eyes came back to me and he smiled. "Well, all right. One favour deserves another. I'll think of something. And tomorrow—at the Holy Year Committee—?"

"Yes."

"I'll bring you the negatives. Goodnight, Father."

"Goodnight."

His face was worried again, and as he turned away I heard him mutter:

"But I just can't think what I'm going to say to the Sub-editor."

Then he was gone. A good man, there are plenty of them. He kept his word.

CHAPTER ELEVEN

The Fag-end Philosopher

How old these children were, far older than I. Their everyday language was fouler than any man's, and their knowledge seemed to reach the limits of all physical experience.

Whiskers, who had witnessed and appreciated my sharp encounter with Fatty, added me to his gang of eight, under the impression, I suppose, that I might be of some use to him. There was one a little older than he—Affoo (Alfonso)—and the others were young and small by comparison. Poor Mangy came along with us as a mascot of whom we were not very proud.

This was the drill. As the night went on, or as the morning began, we collected scraps of paper. Not to make a fire, but to serve as blankets, pillows, mattresses. The fire itself was another matter, and you would be surprised to find how much rubbish in the streets is combustible—garbage and the soles of old boots; and the rinds of oranges and lemons are invaluable once they are dried out, for they are full of oil. As for a piece of cardboard or a cork—or a length of wood fallen from a barrow—!

We usually went to the Maddalena district by way of the Triunfo *pizzeria* and a baker's shop, and we bought ten *lire*'s worth of charcoal. A holed and rusty bucket was our stove, and it was the job of the little ones to get it going.

This district, not far from the bright lights of the station district and its shops, consists of dark little hovels and a labyrinth of lanes. There are no palaces here with porters at the door : nobody asks questions, nobody even sees what is going on. You can feel secure—up to a point. Anyhow in such a place you are far less likely to be disturbed.

Paper mattresses then, which served not very efficiently as insulators against the cold of the stones, and in the midst of our conglomeration of bodies there stood our stove. For lack of solid fuel it would go out in the early hours of the morning, leaving us so numb and frozen that we were forced to get up, to move, to stamp our feet.

At night Whiskers, being our leader, used to lie down first, and then Affoo in the curves of his body. My turn came next and I was tortured by the fact that Affoo had acquired a stray puppy, I suppose partly through a longing for affection and partly as a sort of hot-water bottle. The little creature fidgeted constantly as all puppies do and could never make up its mind where it wanted to be. Having lived in Affoo's shirt in a vertical position for the whole of the day, it could not accustom itself to the horizontal. It climbed and pawed and staggered and slipped and licked everybody's face with indiscriminate love. Nobody had a moment's peace.

Not only that: the warmth of our bodies huddled against one another had brought out the vermin in full force. *Volanti* they are called in *scugnizzo* slang—The Flying Squad—though to me they seemed far more adept at creeping. I still do not know who was responsible for the invasion of this miniature zoo, but I wanted to scratch myself to pieces.

And I could not do so. Not even one covert scratch. As a fully-fledged member of the gang I had to lie still and accept this. For the time being it had to be part of my life.

The puppy, the lice—and for good measure my noisy companion whose head was pillowed on my hip. He coughed and fidgeted and heaved and groaned and I had to reconcile myself to the fact that sleep, under these conditions, was quite out of the question.

Near the Ascolesi hospital there is a fountain in which some of us washed in the morning—but by no means all. The smallest of the gang saw no point in it. Water was not merely cold but it was also wet: and besides, why bother with it when you got dirty all over again?

Then came the main business of their day—the collecting of cigarette-butts.

You cannot realise how important they are. Very often cigarettes are the *scugnizzo*'s main source of income. Drop one in the street, stub it out against a wall or throw it from the window of your car, and this careless gesture of which you are hardly aware has an importance in the lives of many people—not only the *scugnizzi* but the unemployed, the beggars, the tramps and the aged who have no family to help them.

Indeed most of those who live off the street and its pickings depend almost entirely on cigarette-butts, and what a tedious and exasperating job they have. Consider it: on an average about four butts, providing that they are good ones, are equivalent to one cigarette. And each cigarette weighs about one gramme. You can work it out for yourself, but to pick up even half a kilo of tobacco you have to stoop at least two thousand times.

Moreover, you must have a well-trained eye and a knowledge of the strategic points. The best are obviously the most frequented, and I recommend the waterfront restaurants of Santa Lucia where people may be kept waiting for a table. Otherwise there are cinemas, bars, night-clubs, gambling dens, tram and bus stops, railway stations and funiculars. Unfailingly profitable are the pavements by such places.

The fag-ends of women are preferable to those of men. Women have longer nails and are apt to hold cigarettes at their finger-tips, also to discard them a little sooner than men. Their butts are always cleaner and usually longer than those of our sex.

Not only by the restaurants but down the whole waterfront of Naples you can pick up some real beauties, also in the Via Roma and along Via Chiaia; and above all when the American Fleet is in, because some Americans seem to be in a highly nervous condition, flinging cigarettes all over the place, and besides, their tobacco will bring in two hundred *lire* more per kilo.

There is a technique in collecting butts and everyone has his own method. The most common is to stoop and grab with thumb and two fingers but some can pick them up with their toes or with a damp stick, or even with a pin on the end of a cane : a most sophisticated approach to the problem. As to the time of day or night, it is as well to avoid the peak traffic hours, for it can be a hazardous business snatching a butt from under three Fiat Millecento abreast followed by a lorry, a *carrozza*, and five motorbicycles.

I remember with astonishment that some people I knew who had organised a dormitory for the homeless could never understand why so many tramps preferred to spend their night on the street instead of enjoying a clean and comfortable bed. The answer was perfectly simple. They would have had to be indoors by nine o'clock, a time when fag-end collecting, the only source of their meagre income, was about to begin.

This sort of stupidity, this utter incomprehension of how people live their lives and when and where they live them is exactly the kind of thing I have had to fight all my life. Goodness in a vacuum of ignorance is of no value at all. For me, goodness is a physical force which must be harnessed to life as we find it. That street lamp is nearer to us than the stars.

But to return to our cigarette-butts, as indeed we always did—I found that I had learned the habit of looking at the pavement, the road, the gutter. I knew several lads who had acquired a sort of curvature of the spine as a result. It becomes automatic, irresistible : you stoop and pounce. I did it at first experimentally and then instinctively. In an unguarded moment I can still do it.

And as for the tobacco trade, let me give you some facts and figures.

Cleaners of cinemas and theatres are of course entitled to all the butts they find on the floor, and they, together with barmen and with porters from blocks of offices bring the morning's gatherings to the "market", unless they need them for their own use. Those who live by this trade make up parcels of the mixed tobacco, which they sell for sums ranging from ten to a hundred *lire*, and their haunts are the steps of the cinemas near the Porta Capuana, the central railway station, and the Museum.

You need to be a smart bargainer, or you'll be cheated. One boy confided to me that he had sold half a kilo of tobacco for as little as fifty *lire*—though I think he must have been exaggerating for at his age he could not possibly have picked up more than 300 grammes in one evening. Even so, he should have been entitled to about 350 *lire*, for the price varies between 1300 and 1600 *lire* for one kilogram.

Stubs that have been extinguished between finger and thumb in an office ashtray are worth more than most because they contain more tobacco; whereas those left to die out by themselves are too full of ash. The quality of tobacco, and the difference between Italian and foreign brands, can be detected easily by smell.

As always happens, "larger fish eat smaller fish", and the top racketeers in the trade do very nicely, thank you— unscrupulous types they are, feared by their underlings.

Just imagine it: about a thousand *scugnizzi* and other down-and-outs manage to earn by these back-breaking methods the miserable sum of 500 *lire* a day—something like 6s. 3d. in English money, or call it as much as one American dollar.

But add it all up and you find that the trade brings in an average of half a million *lire* a day or fifteen million a month. In the course of a year we reach the almost incredible figure of one hundred and eighty millions.

(Let me say now that filter-tips, which I confess to smoking myself, are a real menace to the whole industry.)

Tobacco, tobacco, tobacco, and you can well imagine that the *scugnizzo* himself becomes an addict. To smoke is a physical necessity although most butts are a rank and horrible mass of concentrated nicotine. But pleasures are few and this is a momentary solace. You must drug yourself to forget the pavements even for a few seconds, and to forget last night. How can you possibly stop? After six months of smoking sticky fag-ends I myself was as bad as any of them. So were the workmen tumbling out of buses, tired-eyed, in the early morning: never did they buy "tailor-made" cigarettes but always stub-tobacco from which they could make their own.

And there is one other thing you should know.

This industry is strictly illegal in Italy because it competes with the State Monopoly. The police can confiscate all stub-tobacco wherever they can find it, to the misery and rage of those who have spent arduous hours picking it up.

Never shall I forget the sobs of one little lad whose entire collection, one evening's harvest, was whisked away from him by a policeman, nor my own fury when I saw this wretch selling the confiscated tobacco to a dealer round the corner.

In my time I have seen many a rat at close quarters, and I would far rather look at one than at that man's face. Rats have better eyes.

CHAPTER TWELVE

How Not to Steal a Wallet

I must draw some distinctions between my feelings as a vagabond and my feelings as a priest, and I think that they may surprise you.

As a vagabond I had a sense of privilege and freedom—even a kind of diplomatic immunity—because in these clothes and with these companions I could behave in any way I liked without attracting comment or even notice. If I had stood on my head or turned a cartwheel, nobody would have seen me. The whole range of human antics and human behaviour was open to me. Anything was to be expected. And everything was to be learnt. Nobody had secrets any longer.

Whereas a priest is in a very different position, since people think they know exactly what he is and what he wants and instinctively adapt their behaviour and even their language to their own misconception of him. They are never quite at ease : they feel they have to censor themselves and put on imaginary gloves. A priest, they think, is "outside life", and therefore they cannot possibly discuss life with him, never supposing that he could help them to live it. No, he "wouldn't understand". And under the circumstances, of course, how can he hope to do so?

Sometimes the barrier seems almost unbreakable. Even in their reverential greetings such as the kissing of hands—a gesture which always makes me think of naphthalene—people are instinctively defending themselves against us. *"He kisses the hand who cannot bite it"* say the Arabs; a harsh phrase perhaps, but I think I know what they mean. Personally I dislike having my hand kissed and would far rather stand on my head or turn a somersault.

You will see now what my feelings were, living two lives in complete contradiction to one another. On one hand the freedom of the jungle : on the other a well-fitting glass case to shelter one from the dust of real life.

I could not bear it. I had to know, I had to understand why people behave as they do. I had to graze in forbidden fields. For the sake of my conscience I tried to restrict myself to the *fringe* of criminal activities, giving as convincing a performance as I could in order to make my companions believe that I was with them, but I confess—and may the Church forgive me—that now and again I did find myself involved in proceedings that were none too savoury. You cannot always be sure of the exact limits of a situation. Things get out of hand.

And so one day, taking a tram that went to the public baths, I was concerned indirectly in the theft of a wallet. Concerned because I happened to know the two thieves, who winked at me as soon as they boarded the tram, thinking perhaps that I had the same intentions. I knew perfectly well what would happen. I could have raised an alarm but I didn't. Frankly, I wanted to see how things went.

One was a petty thief of some experience and the other his accomplice. And there was I, a possibly useful third. If things went wrong and a wallet had to be passed twice over, I might easily find myself the recipient of it.

Every pickpocket is as superstitious as a servant-girl, and these two before going to "work" were whispering an invocation to the saint whose shrine lit up their alley, as though saints were delighted to assist one Christian in preying on another.

Then at once they began a covert inspection of the anatomy and clothing of their fellow passengers, assessing with clinical precision the whereabouts of any pocket and the nature of its contents.

They had chosen a good hunting-ground, for the tram was crowded and the noise considerable. Seeing them edge their way very gradually forward, as all Italians must—having entered by the back door and paid your fare you have to move as best you can up to the front exit—I could not help wondering in fascination mixed with apprehension exactly whom they were going to choose as their victim. They seemed so completely at ease, not glancing at one another though well aware of each other's slightest movement: indeed, they seemed more interested in the advertisements or in looking out of the windows. I could hardly bear the suspense. And then I saw that they had reached their quarry, for the "sandwich operation" had begun. These two had wedged themselves behind and in front of the best-dressed man in the tram.

It would happen at any moment. My heart was pounding and my face went scarlet. A plump housewife of about forty, almost forced against me by the pressure of the crowd, mistook the reason for my blushes and took the opportunity to move a little closer: perhaps my stubbly chin had excited an interest in her that was not entirely maternal—she cannot have been fascinated by my clothes.

And there, further on, was Operation Sandwich about to begin. The wallet (in underworld slang O Lasagne, after a kind of macaroni) had undoubtedly been located. Why do we ever carry them in our hip pockets? All that is needed is a neat little slash with a razor blade, and out pops O Lasagne like a bird released from its cage.

In this case not the experienced thief but his disciple-accomplice, who was evidently being taught his job, was to wield the razor. And then I grew critical. But how clumsy he was, how slow, like somebody fishing under water! Really, that would never do . . .

He bungled it horribly. I don't know if he was too nervous or if somebody jerked his arm or if the tram lurched at the critical moment, but the neat cut turned out to be a heavy gash that cut right into the man's bottom.

One yell and he jumped as though stung by a swarm of

bees, clapped his hand to his rear, found it covered in blood, and yelled again.

There was the wildest confusion in which the wallet was of course quite easily passed. Nobody knew what had happened. Somebody could have been murdered. The tram stopped and everybody got out hastily, for nobody wanted to be involved with the police. In the meantime my interested housewife had flung her arms round my neck and fainted, but I managed to present her to the conductor as I left.

The master thief—the "hen" as they are called—was nabbed by a police agent at once but there was nothing to be found on him, for he had contrived to slip the wallet back again.

We all went off in different directions, but in a little while I found the inexpert accomplice following me—thinking, I suppose, that I was a bird of his kind. I glanced at him contemptuously.

"Messed things up, didn't you?"

An understatement; but it was sometimes as well to be critical.

"I don't know so much. Got the wallet, didn't I, though I know I carved him harder than I meant."

When we had gone a little further he produced his prize. In it there was an identity card—a *documento* with photograph which all Italians have to carry. While I was looking at it he took out other things—probably snapshots and receipts for dry-cleaning or for registered letters—which he carefully stuffed down a drain.

And then he swore vigorously.

"What's the matter?"

He was stamping with rage.

"One bastard thousand *lire* note!" he said. "Imagine it—imagine carrying a wallet just for that! Only *one—here, give me that identity card!*"

He snatched it out of my hand, spat lustily into the face of the man he had just robbed and slashed, and tore the photograph into the smallest pieces.

I have always thought that was a perfect illustration of the phrase "adding insult to injury".

CHAPTER THIRTEEN

Getting Away with It

Those two were regular pickpockets: it was their profession and in all likelihood it still is.

But except in a few rare cases the *scugnizzo* himself is not a pickpocket, and I have met only one who had the remarkable accomplishment of extracting wallets with his toes. The *scugnizzo* is not a confirmed thief in that he does not deliberately adopt thieving as a profession. He will steal, of course, but he will steal only what comes handiest and what he desperately needs in order to continue his existence.

His pilfering is generally confined to the fruit-stalls or fish-markets: the former produce he is apt to start eating almost before he is out of sight, because he is so hungry: and the latter he carries about in a *spasella* or open basket, to sell to the first client he can find.

I cannot help laughing when I think of little Franchetiello and his methods. Whenever he went to the fruit market he used to tie his trousers to his ankles with string and slip all the fruit he could lay hands on through the holes in his pockets. In the end he could scarcely walk, for his legs were as thick as Greek columns : but once he managed to waddle round the corner there was fruit for us all.

Sea-fruit we might lack, but never that of the orchards while he was about. And he was an expert too in whisking packets of cigarettes from the open stalls, under cover of asking how much they cost. His bony hand came down on a packet while with index finger and thumb he pointed out what interested him, asking the price. With the three remaining fingers he would palm what lay beneath his hand, and under the eyes of the vendor. Others tried doing this, but they were far less expert at it and in the end they ruined his chances. Packets of cigarettes began to have wire netting over them as though they were in a hen coop, and you could inspect but not touch them.

Yes, of course the *scugnizzo* will steal whenever he gets the chance, but his stealing is never regularly organised. If in the cinema he finds his neighbour asleep he is quite capable of removing his shoes or rifling his pockets and if a gullible countryman appears at the station he will fleece him with gusto. But it is all on the spur of the moment. If a chance arises he grabs it : but he never goes in search of it. The most famous black-market street in Naples, the Forcella, running from Via Duomo down to the old Greek walls of the city, narrow, crowded, noisy, cluttered with stalls of every kind, is always a tremendous temptation to the *scugnizzo*. This is a sort of gastronomical kasbah, the centre of all smuggled goods, chiefly American. Wonderful tins of edibles, bottles of whisky with the right labels (I do not vouch for the contents), cigarettes of any kind but Italian, flints for lighters, fruit, the rich and varied fish of the Gulf, vegetables, barrows of hideous china—all these things are there in glittering quantities, and you nearly knock over a stall in trying to edge by it. All venders are shrieking their wares at the tops of their voices and their pronunciations of some American or English brand-names would be incomprehensible to Americans or English.

One day a grocer in the Forcella had made a massive display of American canned meat, the tins piled carefully on top of one another—it must have taken him a long time— and the result was a pyramid of really impressive dimensions. But our little Pollice (Flea), one of the regimental mascots, decided that morning to sample the results of Allied Collaboration (not that we Neapolitans were ever reluctant to do so) and I confess my sympathies were with him. Looking at that monument of meat I could not help wondering if one can of it would ever be missed, and the thought of buying a sandwich to stave off my hunger became less and less attractive.

Unfortunately Flea grabbed what must have been the cornerstone of the whole edifice, for the pyramid breathed, wavered, gave a sudden lurch and started to crumble like an unstable family of acrobats in a circus, one tumbling on another and finally falling to the ground in a devastating

crash—and the cans, being round, hurtling off in all
directions.

The passers-by howled with merriment. We ourselves,
with the exception of Flea, were at first rooted to the spot,
fascinated by what had happened. The grocer went raving
mad. In vain did I try to persuade him that the rest of us
would pick them all up again, and when I myself darted
after a can that seemed to have acquired a life and purpose
of its own the grocer rushed after me with oaths, under the
impression that I was going to make off with it. If I had
not torn myself away from him I would have been beaten
up. It was clearly time for us all to disappear.

When we finally found little Flea he had managed to
open the can and was now licking from his fingers the
savoury jelly that had surrounded the meat; like a bear cub
that had just emptied a full jar of honey.

But on another occasion he became involved with a bottle
of milk, and the results were less successful.

In Naples the morning milk is not left on the doorsteps
of houses except in the most respectable areas. However, at
an early hour one milkman did leave a large bottle, a
gleaming white litre, outside a house that was a little superior
to its neighbours in a dilapidated district: either he was
tired of knocking and waiting for the door to be opened, or
else he had left it there safely before.

Flea stood looking at that solitary bottle and it must have
seemed to look back at him, asking for an owner. Anybody
could snatch it—what a fool of a milkman to leave it
about!—and in his fear that somebody else might whisk it
away or that a boy older than himself might challenge him

for possession of it, he clasped it to his bosom and ran, a seven-year-old child with a bottle nearly half the size of himself.

But he ran in the wrong direction. Slap into the arms of the milkman as he came round the corner. One startled bellow, a hefty clout, and down fell Flea with his bottle, both of them in tears, for a pool of white began to spread on the pavement. Cuffs and curses rained down on the frightened child, and at last the milkman went off on his rounds, still shouting with anger.

Alone again, sobbing, the boy stretched out his hand to the good milk and began to dip, tasting at last what he had so much wanted and needed, and repeating the pathetic gesture until the milk was good no longer but growing muddier and muddier as it mixed with the dirt of the pavement. But he still went on, reluctant to finish, for he had paid for it with blows and misery.

*　　　*　　　*　　　*

To steal food or drink when you are hungry or thirsty—especially when you are so young that you are always one or the other, if not both—is surely most understandable. What small boy ever passes an orchard without looking to see if there are apples within reach, even when he has been well fed? And here were the *scugnizzi* pilfering in order to survive.

I had less sympathy for the past exploits of Palluottolo, who came to us one night. At the age of seventeen he had stolen several wallets, a pair of shoes and a camera. You do not steal on that scale merely for survival, but to buy some flashy clothes, take a girl to the cinema and fling your weight about as long as the money lasts. But his high-life was short lived and the police caught up with him—that was why he joined our camp. And he was by no means the only young thief "on the run" who sought refuge with us, glad to be in the company of lesser thieves and to know that they had an intuitive capacity for scenting the whereabouts of the police.

His young face wore a perpetual grimace of low cunning that was sometimes irresistibly funny, and as he was with us for six months, having made the station and the Vasto districts too hot to hold him, we had plenty of opportunity to enjoy it. I must say for Palluottolo that during that time he behaved himself, laying hands on no more than was strictly necessary for his daily existence—and the little that he took he was ready to share with those hungrier than he.

I remember that one night when our larder had been emptier than we could any longer bear we all began to wander towards the Tribunali district in the hope of improving matters. Somehow the lights and the glittering tram-lines seemed to warm us a little—and how cold you are when hungry, even when there is no chill in the air! Shop windows or bars that are lit are encouraging too and you want to put out your hands to them. But best of all—a miracle and a torture—is an open bakery, cooking through the night.

This was a busy one, for loaves for the whole district were being brought out of the oven, golden and fresh, crisp, crackly and hot, beautiful even to look at, infecting the whole street with their delicious presence. Bread—the symbol of all food from times of antiquity—but bread here and *today*. Bread is primitive, and so are man's reactions to it.

We began closing in. I cannot help thinking that our eyes must have glowed like those of cats, so intent were we, so concentrated on what we saw and smelt and wanted with our whole being; but the bakers were busy with their long wooden shovels and did not seem to notice us. Nobody made a sign : there was no need : we all knew. For our mouths must have been watering enough to put out the ovens.

It happened in a split second, and we were all running frantically after Palluottolo, whose legs were a little longer than most of ours. Behind us there was a babble of voices invoking the saints in none too reverent a fashion. In front of us was a figure rushing towards the Via Forcella and its alleys. As I caught up with him he hurled something at me as though he were passing a ball on a football field. It was warm and crisp.

Give us this day, O Lord, our daily bread . . .

This day I took it from the hands of a thief.

*   *   *   *

I was sorry when Palluottolo went. After six months the police found him and that mischievous smirk was no longer to be seen. He probably went to gaol and learnt from older prisoners even worse rackets than he had previously known. He would have been far better off with our gang.

It is strange, I admit, to think of the *scugnizzo* as a reforming influence.

CHAPTER FOURTEEN

Always
on the
Move

We were all sitting on the ground behind the Iris Cinema, near the station. Little Flea, knowing his duties, had got the bucket fire going and it cheered us and lit our faces and made us open our mouths more freely. It was always the gang's custom at such a time to talk about the adventures of the day, embellishing and exaggerating of course, and using as many oaths and obscenities as possible. I was suddenly startled by hearing my "name".

"And what did *you* do, Naso Stuorto?"

"Wouldn't you like to know."

"I can guess."

"So can anybody."

At these moments (which I always dreaded) I took refuge in the pungent phrases of the thickest Neapolitan slang, which it is practically impossible to translate—even into ordinary Italian. It was my only refuge, my only way of keeping my end up, of saving my face with them. Sometimes I could make them burst out laughing with it, and it would often retrieve the situation by making them forget what they had asked me. But tonight they seemed to be insistent.

"Come on, now" said Whiskers. "You're the only one who talks so much without saying anything. It's about time you opened your mouth a bit wider."

A small boy, a newcomer, drew closer to me with his eyes aglow. Nobody knew anything about him. He was obviously better dressed than any of us. He had spent the evening listening to us, half-horrified and half-fascinated by everything that we had to say. He was almost too attentive: clearly a strange new world was being revealed to him, and I expect he hoped that I would turn out to be the worst monster of the lot.

What on earth could I say? That I had been on a tram—which was perfectly true—and from which they would draw their own conclusions? But they were all after lurid details of course, and would want to know exactly how much I had picked up and by what methods. Should I show them, in silence, the few *lire* in my pocket? How could I satisfy my conscience and my need to remain a member of the gang? How could I temporise?

I opened my mouth, quite uncertain as to what would come out of it. And at that moment there was an uproar which made us all jump nervously to our feet.

"There he is!" A middle-aged man was running down the street towards us. "Caught you at last, you little devil!"

The small boy instinctively covered his head as though he knew only too well that there would be blows rained on it. And they came down unmercifully. His cries were of such pain that we had to try and rescue him, not understanding the reason for this sudden assault, and the man found himself in the middle of a struggling mass.

"You give him to me!" he yelled. "*He's my son!*" We drew back in silence as the boy collapsed at his father's feet. "How can I help hitting him? Two whole days I've been looking for him. I've walked all over Naples looking for him."

For a moment the man's face was contorted with worry and exhaustion. Then anger got the better of him and he dragged his son away from us. They were still within hearing when the music started all over again.

A painful scene, but its aftermath seemed almost worse; for it was quite clear that the younger ones had been seized with a sort of morbid excitement and had actually enjoyed being witnesses of the attack.

I had already noticed in them an inclination to sadism, and later I came to observe it more carefully. Apart from a delight in hitting those weaker than themselves (which after all can be found in the best schools in any part of the world) there was a deeper, more deliberate, more considered form of cruelty, a desire to inflict pain which can have had no origin except in the abnormalities of their early childhood.

Throwing stones at cats and rats was one of their sports, and when they killed a few they were triumphant.

Some would take a delight in preventing their companions from sleeping, and when a boy could hardly keep
his eyes open they would nudge or cuff him or throw things
at him to keep him awake. They would even set a quantity
of paper ablaze in order to startle him into sitting up
suddenly, and I have also seen them take pleasure in burning
the soles of a boy's feet.

Since poor Mangy would rather do anything than bare
his head to show his scabs they would steal his cap and
hide it, refusing to return it until he was reduced to tears
and despair.

If a victim of their "practical jokes" rebelled and reacted
with spirit they would hit him all the harder, and if he were
tough and plucky they could be merciless.

You can well imagine how the spectacle of a small boy
being beaten by his father excited them that night. They
were restless and became so quarrelsome that we decided
to break up the party and meet later in the Vasto district.

*　　　*　　　*　　　*

Behind the Triunfo *pizzeria* I came across a lad stretched
out on the steps of a house of ill-fame. Michele, a member of
an older gang, had drunk too much wine, and he lay on his
back with mischievous eyes blinking up at the sky. They
would soon close in sleep. And waiting anxiously for them
to do so, a *scugnizzo* hovered in the shadows.

My presence was obviously most unwelcome, but I felt
disinclined to remove it. As usual, I wanted to see what

happened. The *scugnizzo* and I stared at one another for a few moments. Then he said sullenly :

"I got here first."

"All right, you got here first."

"So I don't see why you should have anything."

"What were you after?"

"His money, his boots, and his fags."

We both looked at Michele, who had started to snore. The *scugnizzo* glanced back at me, as though assessing my power to take from him what he regarded as his lawful prizes. Then he added :

"I tell you what. You can have the fags, but I want the money and the boots."

"You can have the fags as well."

"Don't you want *anything*?"

"No."

He was amazed. Then delighted. Then suddenly suspicious.

"But you'll tell. Then I'll get beaten up for it."

"I shan't tell."

In no time at all Michele's pockets were empty and his feet bare. So happy was the *scugnizzo* that he gave me a parting present—a home-made cigarette called a *spiniello*, filled with fag-end tobacco.

I too made a quick exit, for Michele, even when sober and with boots on his feet and money in his pocket, could be a tough customer.

*　　　*　　　*　　　*

That night as indeed on many nights we were always on the move. And there seemed to be a succession of disasters or near-disasters that depressed and unnerved us.

The restaurant in the Via Firenze had no scraps for us this time, but a few were collected from the hotels near the railway station and stored in a large can. I nearly knocked it over, tottering with fatigue in shoes that kept tripping me up, and so furious was the gang that I could have been lynched. It was some while before tempers cooled down and we could sit and eat our supper.

Immediately afterwards we were off again in the hopes of changing our sleeping quarters, as it was becoming impossible to spend the night in the Maddalena district. You needed to be quiet about it, and the little ones kept making so much noise that last night the tenant of an upper floor had been awakened by their din. Down she came flourishing a big broom and threatening to brain the lot of us with it if we didn't clear out. We took to our heels, and after holding a council of war a little further on decided that in future we would try one of the many bombed-out houses along the waterfront.

So here we were, a band of refugees in our own city, making for the sea. Whiskers and I went on ahead and were joined by Affoo of the Puppy—three seniors leading a small rabble of exhausted children. Supper, such as it was, seemed to have stimulated Affoo for he suddenly launched out into a little speech, as though we were a committee discussing the club rules.

In future no seniors should go round begging cast-off clothing from respectable houses. It was beneath their dignity! That matter should be left to the little ones, and anyway they always got more sympathy. As for cleanliness (I was so startled to hear it even mentioned that I listened in fascination) we as seniors should wash as often as possible (I had been at close quarters with Affoo) and try to get rid of our insects. And the little ones must be taught—

He suddenly stopped and nudged me.

"What a beauty!" he exclaimed. "Oh, what a beauty!"

I turned to see what had excited him. It was a well-arranged shop-window with nothing remarkable about it.

"Quite pleasant" I said, stupidly. I should have known that Affoo was not discussing aesthetics (though after hygiene anything seemed possible) but was merely looking at it with a shoplifter's eye.

When we reached the gates of the docks and wharves we found the guards on duty eyeing us with suspicion and discussing us, so we moved to the darker side of the road. But only to run into two policemen.

"What are you boys doing down here at this time of night?"

"Looking for somewhere to sleep."

"Why don't you sleep where you usually do?"

"Somebody's pinched our place."

There were far more questions to come.

"What's your name? How old are you? And you? What d'you do to pick up a living?"

The others did not seem to be too much alarmed by this interrogation, but for me it was an unbearable torture. Not only because I might have difficulties with the police but because my real identity might come out at any moment in front of my companions—and all my months of work with them would be lost. They would never let me come near them again. Gone would be my chance of reaching that stage—and how carefully it had to be considered, how well timed!—when I could reveal to them that their companion of so many nights was also a priest.

My mouth went dry and I felt even physically sick. At a distance I heard somebody saying :

"Well, you see, we just do what we can. They give us grub at a few places—you know, hotel kitchens and such— and then, well, for the rest of the time we just pick up cigarette butts. We can sell them—"

"Yes, I know about that. So all you're after is a place to sleep, eh?"

"That's all."

"Well, be off with you, then. But mind you give me no trouble. Because I'm telling you this—if you're a nuisance to me *I can be far more of a nuisance to you!*"

"Yes, Sergeant. Goodnight, Sergeant."

It was finished. As I walked on with the group I was trembling all over.

*　　　*　　　*　　　*

Acres of rubble. Crumbling weed-tufted doorways of what had once been patrician palaces. Here and there the beginnings of hideous and unsavoury shanty-towns formed of small, flimsy and highly inflammable shacks built sometimes of cardboard held together with sticks, incapable of keeping out the weather. Here people lived, and in the cellars of bombed buildings that they shared with rats. It was grotesque, macabre—and also pitiful, for I could not help feeling that the *scugnizzi* themselves had sometimes fared better than these families.

We climbed under a battered triumphal arch to find ourselves in a roofless hall. The walls were still standing, but it seemed unwise to go near them—indeed to bump against anything in that sinister darkness might lead to a complete catastrophe. And the stench of decay was in any case unbearable.

Once again we were forced to withdraw, the little ones blaspheming to the sky because it was so late and we had not yet found them any sleeping quarters. We had to make the humiliating decision to return to the Maddalena district, hoping not to encounter another tenant with a broom, or at least not such a formidable one: and in any case by the time we arrived there the children would be so worn out that they would drop asleep without a sound.

As we trudged back Affoo began to make plans for the next night. We would start early and organise ourselves properly in a place near the fish-market—cover the ground with pieces of tin, get our fire-bucket going, collect plenty of paper . . .

The others may have been encouraged by his chatter, but it made me ache with longing for Materdei which would soon be ready to receive them. To give them beds, to give them a roof, to give them warmth, clothing, food! Not tomorrow night, nor even next week, but soon, soon!

Very few hours were left before dawn and they passed with only one further incident: an encounter with the bootless, tobacco-less and penniless Michele in a drunken rage and smelling far worse than the whole lot of us put together. But he was so unsteady and so incoherent that we could easily shake him off, pretending not to understand what he was talking about.

And so ended A Neapolitan Night's Entertainment.

*   *   *   *

At seven o'clock the next morning I was wondering how I could possibly shake off Affoo, who insisted on walking with me to the tram stop. On the way we passed a brand-new Fiat Millecento standing unattended by the kerb, and again he nudged me.

"What d'you want a tram for? We could knock this off easily."

"Affoo, are you crazy?"

I must not lose my temper. And I must catch my tram.

For it was Sunday morning and my workmen were expecting me. I did not want to keep them waiting for Holy Mass.

CHAPTER FIFTEEN

The "Scugnizzo": An Analysis

Now let me put on my soutane again and look at the *scugnizzo* from inside it.

If anyone had watched me as a priest, walking down the street with an abstracted air or standing contemplatively at a bus stop, he might have wondered what religious meditations were occupying my mind. But I confess that in all likelihood I would be studying the extraordinary lessons that the nights had taught me—trying to understand the patterns of *scugnizzo* behaviour, and discovering to my surprise that there were many different kinds of *scugnizzi*. Wondering why this was so and what would be the reasons for their differing. Recalling what I had managed to learn of their family backgrounds, searching for the roots from which they had sprung. Noting where the types overlapped, and where they were completely at variance. Asking myself what conclusions I could draw, and if I were capable of a dispassionate and useful analysis.

I would be thinking too of other strange lessons I had learnt, which seemed to make such a mockery of life as it is conventionally lived. That cleanliness can be a luxury: that street refuse is potential warmth in winter: that a watch is unnecessary: that the smoker does not need to buy cigarettes: that a discarded crust of *pizza* or a handful of coffee-grounds can be regarded as food: that public transport is free, so long as you can hang on.

The average man lacks the simple imagination to know how to live as we lived. Often our lives seemed to begin where his left off.

As an urchin I could sit where I pleased, eat where I pleased, sleep on the pavement or in the bottom of a boat without fear of soiling my clothes. I could blow my nose in the gutter (which the Japanese, a fastidious people, think far more sanitary than blowing it in a handkerchief which you then keep in your pocket). I could scratch myself in all possible places without anyone knowing or caring. I could wander through notoriously vicious and dangerous spots without the slightest fear of molestation, my rags for my passport.

It is a life in which the weakest becomes the strongest. You have already won because you have nothing to lose. Here, only the rich man is weak, because he is open to attack on all fronts.

And so I could look at the night-world from the day-world, trying to see far beyond my own reflection in it. Trying, without emotion, to discover why this child and that and the other had come to sit down by a bucket fire in the middle of the night and to spend his days in picking up cigarette-butts.

*   *   *   *

I came to the conclusion that one could distinguish two main groups of *scugnizzi* whom, for want of better terms, I would loosely describe as professionals and amateurs.

The professionals are by far the larger group and contain several subdivisions, so let us take them first.

Complete self-sufficiency is the chief characteristic of the true professional. He has no parents or relatives, and answers to nobody but himself. He must solve unaided the daily problems of existence. It is as though he has been created to be exactly what he is now, half-child and half-man and yet neither. Like all Neapolitan people he is sentimental by inheritance and has an innate longing for affection, but as this is something he has never been given, he does not consciously miss it. He therefore suffers less from resentments and frustrations than other types, the products of broken homes. He is vivacious, bold, quick and adaptable, and you know exactly where you are with him. He is, in fact, the most likeable of them all.

Whereas the *scugnizzo* with only one parent who is unable to feed him or give him any upbringing is in quite a different category. He is a sad creature, moody, stranded, lost, always searching for something which is never to be found. A very fine thread links him to what might have been a home, and soon he will break it in despair.

Those who have one parent and a stepfather or step-mother are hurt and betrayed and uncomprehending. Generally the step-parent has children of his or her own who are treated better than he and given the larger share of affection. He is born an inferior, and has a grudge against life itself.

There is also the *scugnizzo* whose mother or father is living with an extra-marital partner. The boy's presence becomes a nuisance and an embarrassment. He senses this only too easily, and takes the first opportunity to remove himself.

Again, there is the boy whose father has left home to live with another woman, leaving his mother with the problem of going out to work to support her family. She has no time to look after them : she is worn out, and in a perpetual state of resentment against her runaway husband. The boy is free to pick up any other street urchins he can find, who teach him easy ways of adding to the family budget—and even how to be economically self-sufficient. This is soon followed by a psychological self-sufficiency, and the damage is done.

I have even known cases of a boy with two legal parents and two putative ones—the mother living with another man and the father with another woman. The situation is beyond his understanding. All he knows is that he is somehow an outsider and that he cannot hope to fit into this pattern. And so he leaves.

Not moral but sheer material poverty is sometimes the reason for a boy becoming a *scugnizzo*. So poor are his parents that they are forced to ask him to contribute to the modest budget, and even to become self-supporting. At this stage he is in the amateur category, for he still returns to his home at night. But it happens inevitably that he begins to feel his own importance and to realise that his parents are waiting for the money he can bring back to them. A process of reaction begins. In his childish mind his parents are seen as the robbers of the fruits of his labours, and he comes to the conclusion that he is more exploited than loved. There is an emotional crisis, and he runs away.

Finally, there is a strange category of professional *scugnizzi* who can only be described as pathological cases. They have good parents, homes and affection, and yet they suddenly abandon them for the life of the streets. Why? They are fortunately rare and are extremely puzzling—one cannot hope to explain them in the mass. The most one can do is to examine each case on its merits or demerits and in each, I think, there is an inherent abnormality.

So much for the professionals. The amateurs are far more compact as a group and need less definition.

They are, in the main, the children of lazy and irresponsible parents who pay little attention to them. If a boy is left too much to his own devices he attaches himself to any world which happens to appeal to his imagination. He bears no malice against his parents and is only too happy to be left alone; but contact with the tough veterans of the streets inevitably destroys his innocence. In theory he is not a typical *scugnizzo*, but in practice he lives the same life as they do—excepting that he can wheedle enough money out of his family to pass the whole day in the cinema. He is even allowed to spend the night out of doors with his casual friends, and when at last his parents wake up to the fact that this way of life is leading him to harmful and dangerous habits they try—far too late and with of course no success at all—to exercise some sort of control over him. He reacts violently, for the undisciplined life of the streets has excited him.

An amateur *scugnizzo*. But for how long will he remain an amateur?

*   *   *   *

Children everywhere, children tripping over you, bumping into you, dodging round you—the streets of Naples are always full of children, and it is no wonder that visitors to the city are misled into thinking that they are all *scugnizzi*, which of course is very far from being the truth. If they *were* all *scugnizzi* the problem would be hopeless : it is quite enough to deal with the real professionals and amateurs who together number between three and four thousand. But there is a vast difference between those who live off the streets and those who merely haunt them.

They have always haunted the streets of Naples and always will, for the streets are an integral part of their lives —especially for those born in the *bassi*. And that raises yet another broblem.

The *bassi* are one-room homes opening straight on to the street. In some quarters you can see this room looking spick and span and well cared for. In others it may be dark and unwholesome. In both, the main feature of the room is a large bed, and any other pieces of furniture for which space can be found are grouped round this symbol of The Family. Outside the door—sometimes a half-door, like a horse-box —you will probably find a chicken coop and a festoon of laundry lines, and in summer you will see men playing cards together or lying out in the sun, occasionally on a battered sofa; or groups of women sewing together or preparing meals or washing their clothes out of doors.

You will see now that the street is part of the home: it is a family terrace, it is an extra room. If you try to drive your car through such a street, do not be surprised if you are followed by curses and the shaking of fists, for the place belongs to them, not to you.

Every street and lane has its own particular shrine and its patron saint, which explains why in summer Naples seems to be perpetually in festival. The greatest pride is taken in competing with other lanes in decoration (it is a wonder, sometimes, that the strings of candle-lit lanterns do not burn down the washing) and these small but locally important celebrations give everyone the chance of a few days' holiday, a time for laughter and relaxation, even if it is merely spent at home or sitting in the street.

Do not let me give the impression that the life of the *bassi* has a bad influence on children. Indeed, I am tempted to say that in many ways they benefit from it. Children of other regions are by comparison restricted and confined, absorbing every day the same sensations, seeing the same people, the same images, hearing the same voices making the same remarks, living always indoors. Whereas the child of the street is in the midst of life itself, with its infinite variety of characters, incidents and sensations. He is at the same time spectator and actor in a theatre which provides a multiplicity of non-stop performances, ranging from the sellers of lottery and raffle tickets to the jugglers and puppet-show men, the colourful street-vendors of all types with their varied cries and quick repartee, and above all, as though this were an open stage-setting in which many scenes can be played at the same time, he is a daily witness of the human comedy and can take part in it.

I am not arguing that the *bassi* provide an ideal way of living: I merely point out, for those who wish to abolish them altogether, that at least on the young the effects of street life are far from harmful. The boy of the *bassi* goes to school like any other, and when he is old enough he will work as assistant to the chief grocer or barber in the district. As for his parents—who are living in the *bassi* because they cannot afford to live anywhere else—their ground floor quarters provide them with the chance of carrying on all sorts of petty trades which can be expanded into sources of livelihood.

And they too are devoted to the street. I remember that when the *bassi* of the crowded Market and the Borgo Loreto districts crumbled under the weight of Allied bombs, the surviving inhabitants moved to ancient quarters which had existed under the Spanish occupation, and settled in the narrow lanes above Via Roma and in the Sanità districts —but they never left the street! Wherever they went, they created other *bassi*.

No, do not abolish them. Do something else. Give these people steady work and the chance of living in clean new

houses, from the balconies of which they can still watch
the stream of life that means so much to them.

    *   *   *   *

With children from the crowded rooms of the *bassi*, as of
course with the *scugnizzi* from broken homes whom I described earlier in this chapter, there is always the problem
of far too early familiarity with sexual matters. Where
people in other countries seem to be so concerned about
instruction in the facts of life, at what age it should be
given, by whom, and in what manner, we have instead a
situation in which even the smallest children already know
far too much. There is nothing that they have not heard
about and little that they themselves have not witnessed.

Is it surprising, then, that while they are still children,
and with the hot sun in their blood, they should begin to
imitate their elders? Is it surprising that even incest should
exist? Innocence has been denied them, and morals they
have never been taught.

Indeed, the most painful part of my nights' adventures
has been to hear the filth that came from the lips of even
the youngest, and to see them making obscene gestures. I
once lost my temper with a *scugnizzo* who had turned into
a little *voyeur*. He knew of a quiet spot in a back lane to
which, for a tip, he would lead amorous couples, and
through a well-arranged peephole he and his gloating companions would watch the performance. A child once described it to me with such a sickening wealth of detail that
I could not bear it, and I hit him. How he interpreted the

blow I cannot imagine. He probably thought I was angry at not having seen the spectacle for myself. . . .

*   *   *   *

I have heard many superficial observations about the *scugnizzo*, but there are two in particular that I would like to qualify and correct.

One is that he is physically tough, and that life on the streets has hardened him against weather and inoculated him against illness. Such children do exist—but how many more have no stamina at all and are easily attacked by any kind of disease. How many nights have I lain awake listening to a child with asthma or a hacking cough! As though in the wards of a hospital—where indeed they should have been—I have seen children with swollen lips, eyes burnt with trachoma, heads reddened with scabies or ringworm, calloused and blistered feet. The street may fortify: but it can also consume. Many a boy between fifteen and sixteen has the physique of one between ten and twelve.

Given proper care (and happily I can now vouch for this) such sickly children seem to expand physically within a matter of months, and they grow like plants after rain.

Another popular fallacy is that all *scugnizzi* are sharp-witted. Certainly, the mere need to exist has made them cunning, and as I have already said, they have knowledge beyond their years. But the fact that it is *beyond* their years is important: they have never had time to digest it, being neither children nor men. And indeed I have known many a *scugnizzo* who seemed at first sight to be an imbecile. The many shocks of life had been too much for his unformed personality, and he had shut himself in. (Likewise, stammering and defects of speech are common for various psychological reasons, though they gradually disappear in the face of trust and affection.)

But those "sharp wits", I am afraid, are as superficial as the judgment that all *scugnizzi* have them.

*   *   *   *

There is something to be learnt, too, from watching these boys playing cards. They do not play like any other children I have ever seen—never for relaxation and enjoyment, but with a fierce and bitter concentration, with the intense air of desperate gamblers who have empires to lose. And indeed their little empires of cigarette butts or a few *lire* may well be taken from them : I have many times seen the flush of triumph on the face of the victor, and the shocked pallor of the loser, miserable beyond all proportion to this minor misfortune. Crouched in some dark corner over a feverish game of *zecchinetto* for hours, they will only get to their feet when they have "burnt" their last copper and fag-end. No game is ever played by a *scugnizzo* for its own sake.

I have seen him argue, quarrel, steal and cheat. Contact with all the more brutal aspects of life has taught him that nothing counts but money—and when he sees the activities of his elders he is confirmed in that impression. The ugliest actions are fully justified if they produce money. Money is for him the ultimate aim of existence. It is the final and unanswerable bargaining point.

Which reminds me of one of the cruellest things I have

ever heard said to anybody. A mother was reproaching her son for the depraved life he was leading, and spoke to him gently of the many sacrifices she had made for him. He turned on her in fury.

"All right," he said. "Tell me how many litres of milk you've given me. I'll pay for them. And then we can close the account."

*　　　*　　　*　　　*

As regards religion the *scugnizzi* are not actively hostile but merely indifferent. They are excited of course by saints' festivals, for then the Church comes into their street and there is pomp and colour and singing to stir their imaginations. Some I have heard declare their dislike of priests, whom they despised as men who had simply failed to become anything else, but in the main they are regarded as good-natured, harmless dupes, too wrapped in themselves and their ceremonies to have any real contact with existence.

Had they realised that a priest was sitting among them, intent on studying their characters, their problems, their emotions, their brittle self-sufficiency and their unhealed wounds—they would have been amazed.

Perhaps even the toughest of them could be taught something by a timid elder boy with fair hair and light eyes who had once tried to learn about life from books in a seminary, but had preferred instead to read the stones of the pavement.

CHAPTER SIXTEEN

Drawing in
the Net

"Are you there, Vittorio?"

"Yes, Father. Come in and see what we've done. Mind your cassock!"

Freshly whitewashed walls, smelling of a clean dampness and already drying out in patches. And Vittorio had practically whitewashed himself too: he had made a paper cap like an Italian workman, but his face and clothes were spattered.

"That's better. You've got on splendidly."

"I've got helpers as you see."

He indicated two grinning youths dipping their brushes

in a bucket. It always delighted me when my helpers brought in other helpers. Word was going round. Here was Vittorio, a tall young man with sunken cheeks, born in one of the worst slums in Naples, but now a schoolteacher. And this was how he spent his free time—in helping to reconstruct our little church of S. Gennaro a Materdei. And he had brought in others. And the good Ciccio, at this time still inhibited by Crossed Braces, had helped in the only way allowed him—by telling everybody he met about our project. Another young priest, Pasquale, who had been with him on his first ventures in helping the *scugnizzi*—organising that supper for them and trying to clear Mangy's head —was longing to be my first lieutenant in Ciccio's place. And he would be talking too. There would be others, people would come! But Materdei itself—?

"This is the refectory . . . Father . . . "

Vittorio had begun with enthusiasm but I could hear his voice falter. It was as though he had seen it as a vast beautifully equipped dining room, shining and civilised, and was suddenly faced with it as it really was—a small stark white space furnished with wooden boxes, the "tables" of which had candles on them.

"Well, that's all right for the moment. When d'you think we'll have electricity?"

Vittorio indicated a vague but possibly lethal piece of flex hanging from a corner and a hole in the wall for a junction-box.

"I'm getting on."

"*You*, Vittorio?"

He laughed.

"Don't be alarmed, Father. A friend of mine's an expert electrician, and he helps me too."

"Good. We need everybody."

Soon, soon, I had said to myself the other night. And it was as though I had made a promise to the *scugnizzi*. Materdei. S. Gennaro a Materdei. It must be ready for them before I could be ready myself.

"I'm afraid there's no roof on the kitchen yet."

"Never mind, a little rain won't hurt the soup."

"D'you want to see the dormitory, Father? It's—it's not much of a dormitory yet."

"Let me see."

A pile of blankets—good. Clean, sound walls, bare and negative. And a heap of dry straw.

"That straw," I said, "you must put it into sacks at least. Try to make straw mattresses if you can, for the time being. Later on we shall have real mattresses and real beds."

"But how? Where shall we get the money?"

"Come downstairs, Vittorio, and I'll tell you."

It was getting dark and in the refectory I put a match to one of the candles. This seemed like a celebration to me—perhaps a premature one; but the small light grew and it may have helped Vittorio to see the place again as he had imagined it. We lit cigarettes from the flame and were silent for a moment. There was this clean damp smell. I said :

"Can you get hold of a hand-cart?"

"A hand-cart, Father?"

"Yes, a stout one. We've got to collect scrap-iron. There's plenty to be had for the asking—old bedsteads, the bases of cast-iron sewing machines and mangles, and broken pots and pans. You can even buy scrap-iron in the market and sell it at a profit if you know where to go. It's just a matter of transport."

"Well, yes. Yes, I suppose I could."

"Then later the hand-cart becomes a donkey-cart."

"A *donkey-cart*?"

"And then the donkey-cart becomes a lorry."

"A *lorry*?"

"It grows, you see." I looked round at the candle-lit walls. "It all grows. It's got to grow. We'll make it grow."

"Yes, Father."

I stood up.

"What's the time?"

"Twenty past nine."

"I must go. So many thanks, Vittorio, for all you've done."

"Goodnight, Father."

"*Ciao*."

And an hour later Vittorio could have passed me in the street without recognising me.

*　　　*　　　*　　　*

Another evening I said to him:

"Try it. The Vasto district's the place—they're all there from eleven onwards. See if you can get two or three—"

"But I wouldn't know what to say to them!"

"You, a Neapolitan?"

"I've never talked to *scugnizzi*, Father."

"You've missed something! Anyway, just keep quiet for

a bit—listen to them—and if you get the chance of making a joke, do so. Then give them cigarettes—not before. Then sit down on a step or on the pavement. Then tell them—tell them you know of a place, out of the rain, where they can sleep as long as they want, without fear of the police or of people threatening them with brooms. Tell them they can sleep there every night if they want. Tell them they can be sure of it. Tell them—oh, you'll know what to tell them."

"I'll do my best, Father."

Poor Vittorio—he managed, for all his endeavours, to bring one solitary *scugnizzo* to Materdei : and after a couple of nights the child vanished.

Looking back, I am not in the least surprised. It was far too soon. The house was not merely physically unready, it was not human enough. It needed people. It needed Pasquale. It needed Pasquale's helpers. It needed anybody and everybody who could colour those hard white walls with welcome and affection and understanding. Vittorio was invaluable, but to achieve all this was beyond him.

It was beyond me too for the moment. I could not possibly be in the streets with the *scugnizzi* and at the same time back at Materdei, ready to receive them. Nor could I suddenly appear as a priest in the Vasto district : in the first place they would not have recognised me, and if I had compelled them to do so the shock would have been so great that it would have undone all my work. No, the time was not ripe. That moment would have to be chosen with very great care, perhaps even by intuition.

One must move slowly and cautiously. And the last thing I wanted was that the boys should be coerced. They must come to Materdei because they wanted to come, even if it were only out of curiosity.

But wheels were turning; Pasquale had already presented himself to our parish church as a volunteer helper at S. Gennaro, and he had been accepted. This was wonderful news. He could appear to the *scugnizzi* in the clothes of a priest without arousing any suspicion : he could establish the first contacts with them by night and keep in touch with them by day. And in his enthusiasm for our scrap-iron scheme he had already organised the provision of bedsteads on hire-purchase.

Here was my first lieutenant at last, and here were the beginnings of Materdei. Slowly, carefully, I could begin to draw in the net.

*   *   *   *

Thanks to Pasquale, the empty little church without an altar began to resound with the shouts and laughter of a few children. And as for me, if I were going to draw in that net I must first of all make sure that I had cast it as wide as possible. There were plenty of gangs . . . but of course it would be sensible to begin with my own.

Once again I had to appeal for Salvatore's help, for they knew and accepted him and he was completely at ease with them. He could joke with them and they laughed, he could even insult them and they did not seem to mind. Together we concocted a plan, and together we rehearsed our little comedy. It was merely a matter of waiting for the right moment.

For several nights Salvatore came to visit us, just for half an hour or so. Then one night Whiskers happened to say:

"Better get that fire going, Flea."

"Yes, it's a bit chilly," said Salvatore. And then, looking up at the starless sky: "And I wouldn't be surprised if it rained."

"Winter again," said O Cinese.

"Must be a bad time for you boys. I mean, with nowhere to sleep."

"We always find somewhere."

"Not always," I cut in. "Remember that time when we went from the Vasto to the Maddalena, from the Maddalena down to the docks, and then back to the Maddalena?"

Indeed they remembered it, and the younger ones swore vigorously.

"Generally we find a place," said Mangy. "One place or another."

"Maresciallo"—I called Salvatore by the name the *scugnizzi* had given him—"you told us something the other night."

"About what?"

"Well, about some place we could go, a place with a roof, and we wouldn't have to move."

"Oh, you mean Don Vesuvio's place."

"Who?"

"Don Vesuvio," Whiskers told me. "I remember the name." Then to Salvatore: "Didn't you say there'd be beds?"

"A few, yes, and I believe there'll be more soon."

"What, like a hospital?"

"No, like a house."

"Priests," said Affoo, spitting. "You don't want to get mixed up with *them*."

"It's the police you don't want to get mixed up with, you idiot," said Salvatore. "A priest won't do you any harm."

Affoo was still hostile. A typical *scugnizzo*, he was instinctively suspicious of help. Have you ever tried to feed a wild animal, and have you looked at its eyes?

"Then what's he after, this priest?"

"Nothing," said Salvatore. "He's got room for you, that's all, and food—oh well, if you don't want it—"

"What, food like the Salvation Army?"

"Shelter as well. *Everything*. You'd feel really at home."

It was an unhappy phrase to use, and I knew better than Salvatore how they would react to it. Deep-seated frustrations and resentments came boiling up to the surface. *Home*! In their various ways they thought of home, and with such bitterness. There was a solid, sullen pause. Then Salvatore, realising his mistake, retrieved it very well.

"You all surprise me," he said, "being offered something and not taking it. That isn't like you." He pulled out a packet of cigarettes. "For example, I offer you these, but of course you don't want them."

There was a wild scuffle at the end of which Salvatore was lying flat on his back, roaring with laughter, and every *scugnizzo* had a cigarette in his mouth.

I was laughing too. I said:

"Well, what d'you think about it, Affoo? What about our going to Don Vesuvio's place?"

Affoo merely shrugged. Hostility had given way to a sort of reluctant indifference.

"Whiskers?"

"No harm in trying it, but where is it and how do we get in? People like us?"

Salvatore told them about S. Gennaro a Materdei which, as it happened, was not a great distance from where we were. The boys knew it just as a bombed and crumbling church. They had passed it many times.

"And I'll tell you how you get in," said Salvatore, jumping to his feet. "I'll go there now and get a letter for you. You just hand it in to them at the door. As soon as they see it they'll know who you are. And you'll be welcome."

He went—and the letter was of course already in his pocket. I had written:

Dear Pasquale,

Please do what you can to welcome my fellow gangsters. They are good lads.

Yours, Mario.

We waited. And we waited. And Salvatore did not come back. But what on earth could have happened to him? A street accident—heaven forbid! Or, if he had gone home, some family crisis? An unexpected meeting with friends on the way? Some uncertainty as to where we were? Had he lost the letter or left it behind? There was no accounting for it, but he simply did not arrive.

"You see," said Affoo, "he doesn't come back."

I was upset and bewildered. This net of mine seemed to have broken at the very first pull. Hours went by—though of course I had no means of knowing the time and in my anxiety I may well have exaggerated. But in the end I could bear it no longer and I stood up.

"Look, I know what's happened," I said. "O Maresciallo's just forgotten where we are . . . it was over in the Vasto we saw him last night. But we've got to find him somehow. Let's all split up and go and look for him. Then we'll all meet outside Don Vesuvio's place, and let's hope that one of us has got the letter."

We all went off in different directions and I, disconsolately, towards the Vasto. No, far more than disconsolately: I felt bitter, disillusioned, angry and exhausted. Exhausted not only in body but in spirit. I longed for a clean comfortable bed and utter forgetfulness. I wanted to know nothing more about *scugnizzi* or the nights of Naples. Overwork, lack of sleep, a surfeit of strange experiences—it was all too much, and I could have shouted at the top of my voice, I could have walked out into the middle of the traffic and shouted it, that I was sick, sick, sick of living like this. At that moment everything was false and hostile and evil. Why should I go on in this misery and discomfort while other people, other priests, slept happily and with a clear conscience? Why wasn't *my* conscience clear? I hadn't created the *scugnizzo* problem, had I? And what would I get for my pains? Nothing but criticism and abuse from all sides. I was offending the dignity of the priesthood. I was "soiling my cassock" (oh yes, many times had I had that said to me). I was making a laughing-stock of the Church.

I went on mechanically, trying to walk out my anger and resentment. But one must eat and I was so hungry and I stopped at a stall to buy fifteen *lire*'s worth of cuttlefish soup.

The vendor gave a quick glance at my face. I don't know how I must have looked to him but I think he decided that I was a case of acute starvation. There was little left in his cauldron but he gave me the lot, scooping out the remainder of the mussels and clams.

Oh, how good was that hot soup! And what a power food has over one's emotions! I remembered then how crusts of bread had helped me to stave off fear while the Seminary was being bombed, so long ago. And I felt my anger giving place to resignation. If it was not to be tonight, then another night. The boys knew where Materdei was. We would start again.

Still, the Fontanelle seemed a steep climb to me as I plodded my way up to S. Gennaro, whereas I usually did not notice it. And here I was in my own parish, among people who knew me perfectly well in my cassock and who now did not even look in my direction. They were capable of gossiping all day about nothing, and were so clever in guessing their neighbours' most secret thoughts, yet the scandalous vision of priest dressed as vagabond could pass under their noses and they did not even realise it.

There were too many of them about for my liking and it dawned on me that it must be earlier than I had imagined. My anxiety had indeed misled me : it was not yet midnight : I had misjudged the length of Salvatore's absence.

Why must these people dawdle, would they never go home? I lingered by the heavy iron gates of S. Gennaro a Materdei, wondering what to do. In the daytime these gates were left open, but at night—or at least, after midnight— I could open them with a key. If I fumbled with the lock now, in full view of everybody, it would of course arouse suspicion; and in the clothes I wore I could easily be mistaken for a thief.

This final problem seemed to be one too many, and I felt really exhausted. I was rocking on my feet. There was nothing I could do but ring the outside bell, and of course nobody answered. They were all sleeping the deep sleep of those without anxieties. They had probably been asleep for two hours.

"Is it here?"

I wheeled round, awakened as suddenly as if I had had a bucket of cold water thrown over me.

"Affoo—Barbuso—Franchetiello—!"

Six mischievous eyes and three grins to match. My comrades of the gang had followed me and it was Affoo of all people, the reluctant Affoo, who had come across Salvatore in the Vasto district (I could just imagine Salvatore peering through his glasses) and had claimed the letter from him.

"Yes, this is the place. I've rung once—"

"But they won't let us in?"

"Of course they will. But I suppose they weren't expecting us tonight."

I rang that bell with a force I had not possessed a minute ago. I longed for the trumpets of Berlioz to make somebody open a window.

At last it opened, and one of Pasquale's young helpers put his head into the chilly night and shouted :

"Who's there?"

Then with a shock he noticed the four strangers standing outside, and it woke him up.

160

"Just a minute."

He must have run to tell Pasquale, for in no time at all this good priest, minus collar and even minus shoes, carrying a petrol lamp that not only leaked but stank, came out and let us in.

Darting a quick glance at me, he said:

"Who are you?"

This Pilate-like question kept haunting me. I tried not to look too much at Pasquale, for I knew that he would be nervous and embarrassed. He was a genuine person, sincere and perhaps too guileless to be able to assume, at a moment's notice, the rôle of an actor. I said:

"I'm Mario, Father. You've seen me before."

"Yes, I believe I remember you"—not looking at me.

"I'm sorry if it's late, Father. We wanted to come earlier but—where's that letter, Affoo?—we had to bring you this."

There was a disturbance behind us. Three others had turned up. Unbelievably, the gang was nearly complete! I beckoned them.

"They're letting us in!"

Pasquale was looking at the letter, which of course he already knew by heart. His mouth twitched once or twice and his hands were trembling. Then he smiled at us all and said simply:

"Please come in." And after we'd all shuffled sheepishly into the church he added: "I expect you could do with something to eat."

"Thank you, Father."

But not for me, of course: it must be nearly midnight now and at nine o'clock tomorrow morning I had to say Mass for the tram employees of Croce del Lagno. That good cuttlefish soup must be my supper, and whatever else arrived I must contrive to abandon without being noticed.

In Pasquale's absence I scrounged a cigarette-butt from Whiskers and was about to light it when Franchetiello nearly knocked it out of my hand.

"Not *here*," he said, his large dark eyes full of reproach.

"Why not?"

"Well, the priests mightn't like it."

"What, smoking? I don't suppose it worries them."

"How d'you know, Naso Stuorto? You'd better be careful."

It was bread and jam and apples, all they had, and the others were so ravenous that I do not think they saw me stowing my portion away in a corner.

And then—upstairs. Up to straw mattresses with pillows and blankets. After settling them down I told them I was going to sleep in another room. And after a while I crept out with Pasquale. It was nearly two o'clock in the morning.

I felt his arm round my neck.

"Can you believe it, Mario? They're *here*. Can you believe it?"

Some minutes passed before I could answer him. Then I think I said:

"Yes. I've always believed it."

CHAPTER SEVENTEEN

"D'you
Know
Him?"

After a time that hand-cart became a donkey-cart. We used to tether the good beast to the railings outside the church, which of course delighted the boys, who teased him and played with him. They were happy too when the donkey-cart turned itself into a lorry, for that gave some of them—and still gives them—the chance of a drive round Naples, collecting scrap-iron.

It is in a way the cigarette-butt industry all over again, but of course on a mammoth scale—the gathering of unwanted objects that are a potential source of money. Only help and transport are needed. Sometimes we buy scrap-iron ourselves and sell it at a profit. And regularly we leave empty sacks with the porters of blocks of flats, into which tenants put discarded clothes or shoes or any articles which we can turn into cash.

Within a little while the *Casa dello Scugnizzo* became known, and the parish church, the Community of Materdei, saw and approved and put out hands to us. A young professor at the school where I taught, who was also a journalist, promised to write articles about us. Everybody talked—yes and even the *scugnizzi* themselves. Certain priests, it was said, it was whispered in corners, would give you shelter and food, asking absolutely nothing in return. There was no harm in them at all, and they would even joke with you. (Pasquale had now lost his nervousness and was on the best of terms with everybody.)

In fact, the hazy project that Ciccio and I had discussed in a tram so long ago had become at last a reality. Not without pain and not without thought. But two or three extra *scugnizzi* seemed to Pasquale and me like the beginning of a migration, and we welcomed them. The only trouble was that as our responsibilities increased, so did our debts and our problems. More heads and hands were needed—and even if we pulled Naples to pieces it seemed that we would never find enough scrap-iron to keep us solvent.

I was in a dilemma. If I concentrated on the practical work of organisation we would undoubtedly make faster progress—but it was not yet time for me to leave the alley-ways and I had not cast that net nearly far enough. Neither, it seemed to me, had the moment arrived for me to declare myself to them as a priest. That moment must be prepared and chosen so carefully. There was still a great deal to be done.

However, *scugnizzi* arrived, which was the most important thing of all, and if they increased our debts—well, the bills would have to wait a little longer. It would have been absolutely fatal to say at this stage that we could take no more.

I must confess too in all sincerity that some arrived and some left. This was at first disheartening, even incomprehensible, but after a little while I began to understand and accept it. A *scugnizzo* comes or is brought to us out of the streets—perhaps, let us face it, from mere curiosity or for the pleasure of getting something for nothing. He finds shelter, warmth, food, affection, companionship—but after two or three days he becomes restless. The excitement of the streets (he has been used to them for some years, after all) and the thrill of sheer danger, these things pull at him and torment him and drag him back into the vortex. You can imagine too that he needs time to think things over : he needs to make comparisons. Is it really worth while going to the *Casa*? Free food and shelter, yes, but how does that stand up to what you've left behind?

I am thankful that after two or three days most of them come back to us. They have made their comparisons and in their way they are beginning to establish a scale of values. Some of them are lost for good, of course—there are always the impossible cases. But those who return we do not question : we accept them as though they had never been away from us. Which means mostly that they do not want to leave us again.

165

When they have been with us for some time and *then* suddenly go off on their own, that is another matter. We *do* ask questions—even though the police may have already done so. And if they leave us twice we are not anxious to accept them a third time.

We had one very temporary visitor, and he made me and most of my *scugnizzi* extremely angry.

Remember Palluottolo? He was the smart one who had done so well in cameras and wallets and shoes, and who took refuge with our gang while he was a fugitive from the law. He was finally cornered, and for a few months there was no more Palluottolo.

At the *Casa* of all places he suddenly reappeared, having heard of us of course through the grapevine of the underworld. He claimed food and a bed and asked for new clothes. And I regret to say that we provided him with the very best we had; an American-style jacket, stove-pipe pants and the latest in shoes. They seemed to match his brash conversation.

He was with us that night only. The next morning saw the back of his draped shoulders. I was simply furious about this, and two of us decided to teach him a lesson. A few nights afterwards we haunted the station, where for dubious reasons he was apt to show himself, and we peered into every bar and cinema in the neighbourhood without finding him.

Towards one in the morning I spotted him on the steps of the *Tosca* and we very gradually approached him.

"Palluottolo . . . "

He started and looked from one to another of us.

On the street you use very few words. Eyes are enough and he knew what was coming.

"Leave me my pants," he whispered. "I could flog these for a thousand."

We could not oblige him in that respect and stripped him down to his underclothes, removing even his shoes and socks. He did not argue or even try to stop us, knowing our motives, realising that he was in the wrong; and we left him shivering and dazed, gazing after us with melancholy and I hope a little remorse.

*　　　*　　　*　　　*

And this incident was followed quickly by another. My companion, carrying the spoils of Palluottolo's back and shanks, walked with me to the Porta Capuana and then turned down a side street. It was now nearly two o'clock. I called after him, more loudly than I meant:

"See you tomorrow at twelve."

A few steps further on I was stopped by a nightwatchman.

"What are you doing here?"

"Well—just walking."

"Neapolitan?"

"Yes."

"Live in this district?"

"No."

"Then what are you doing in it?"

"I've told you—walking."

The fellow annoyed me. Rashly perhaps, for I could see that he had a revolver, I decided to bait him. His kind of overbearing officialdom infuriated me and I wanted to make a monkey of him.

"Who are you?"

"Oh, what does that matter?"

"Listen, young man, I want to know your name."

"Why? I don't want to know yours."

He started breathing rather heavily.

"I happen to be a nightwatchman."

"Yes, I saw you were armed—but then, so many doubtful people are, these days. So I must ask you to prove your identity. On, come—surely you know it's the duty of an agent to give his qualifications before asking personal questions?"

The heavily-jowled face was comical in its amazement. A mere vagabond talking to him like this? Then he gave a wry grimace and pulled his identity card out of his hip pocket.

"Take a good look at this before I haul you off to the police."

"They know about me," I said.

"That doesn't surprise me."

Taking my time, I studied the photograph and compared it with his face. Then I handed it back and fumbled for my own.

"Well—here you are. As you see, I'm a priest."

"A . . . a *priest*?"

I told him briefly about my work and in a little while he seemed to understand. But he still looked confused and even a little frightened. I smiled and said:

"You know me now? You'll remember me?"

"Yes, but Father—d'you realise that if you'd tried to run away, if you'd even made a movement, I'd have shot at your legs?"

"Shot at my legs? But why?"

"Somebody just now heard you making a date with another . . . with a *scugnizzo*, and he thought you were both planning a job in the neighbourhood."

If I had lost my head I would have ended that morning in hospital. It was lucky that I was alone, too, or I would never have been able to account for myself.

      *   *   *   *

The night-world and then the day-world: the rags and then the cassock.

I now look back in shame at my performance in school, for I would arrive panting and flustered, half an hour late, and my behaviour must have seemed completely neurotic. My students deserved better of me: I could no longer teach them as they should be taught. The Director glared at me resentfully, and somehow this only made matters worse.

If he had spoken to me in reproach or anger I could have borne it better, but he simply looked at me in silence and I too remained dumb. I should of course have explained matters to him, and all would have been well, but without any word from him I simply could not begin. It was in any case not easy for me to describe in the daytime what I saw at night—the only way to remain sane was to try to keep the two worlds separate. And so I had to endure his eyes on me and was locked in silence. It was painful. That mute reproach was a punishment given by a patient man.

But I must add a postscript, even if I anticipate by several months. When my journalist friend at school finally wrote an article about me in *Il Giornale*—the paper which had wanted to publish photographs of the Salvation Army at work—the Director saw it and came to me at once. He put out both hands to mine and this time his eyes were asking for forgiveness.

"If only I'd known, Don Borrelli! But why didn't you tell me?"

Why indeed? I had only half-explained it to myself, and I could not possibly explain it to him. But it was an overwhelming relief that he knew at last.

As for the Holy Year Committee, which I had to attend in the Royal Palace—opposite S. Francesco di Paola where I had spent my very first night as a *scugnizzo*—I cannot think that under the circumstances I can have been a very effective member, though there were times when the need to speak foreign languages, Spanish or English or German, acted as a stimulus and I was forced to keep my wits about me. Priests were arriving from many different parts of the world, and it was one of my duties to receive them.

I remember that on one occasion, when I had gone to the station to welcome a party of South American pilgrims, the day-world and the night-world seemed to overlap for a few moments. I had arrived too early and was waiting under the arches at the entrance, dressed of course as a priest. Up sauntered a youth whom I had often seen when I was with the *scugnizzi* and who did not recognise me in a cassock. He

was one of those creatures known as "square-ushers"—
pimps in league with all the small hotels and dubious
pensioni of the neighbourhood who were only too willing to
let a room for even an hour to "pick-ups" or travellers in
search of an affair.

"Lonely?"

"Not particularly."

"Waiting for someone?"

"Yes."

"Another priest?"

"Several."

Then, to my amazement, he embarked on a long, even
solemn rigmarole about the effects of the vow of chastity and
the different view of sex taken by Protestant clergymen. He
ended by offering me a room in a small hotel—"convenient,
quiet and comfortable—and above all, they give you a
wonderful blanket."

"Thank you, but I've no wish to go to sleep at a quarter
to six in the evening. And I don't think I need a wonderful
blanket at this time of year."

He burst out laughing.

"Don't know the sort of blanket I mean, do you?"

Frankly, I didn't—I had given the word its usual house-
hold significance. But he made it clear that it had yet
another. Sick of the creature and his innuendoes, I employed
the technique I had once used on that station-tout with the
watches. I let fly in a broad Neapolitan that nearly knocked
him over. Just let him keep clear, I told him, of poor pilgrim
priests who were coming here to see the beauties of Naples
and not those of his sordid little hotels. His chin dropped, he

faltered, made me an obsequious gesture, and then hurried away.

Well, that was something new. Blankets. I had never heard the expression even in my nightly adventures.

I admit that you do not need to dress up as a vagabond to come in contact with the cruder side of life, but it annoyed me that not even my cassock had given me a daytime immunity.

*　　　　*　　　　*　　　　*

Then from cassock back to rags—back to the street lamps or the dim and dubious alleys, back to the petty thieving and the panic escapes from the police.

Our flights from justice were of course a very frequent occurrence and were highly organised. Some *scugnizzi* could produce whistles as long and piercing as factory-sirens, which gave us warning from afar. Off with your shoes, then, and rush into the depths of the darkest and loneliest spots into which nobody would want to pursue you.

The police would arrive in our usual haunts and find nothing and nobody. When their jeeps were at the station we were deep in the Vasto: when they reached the Vasto we were in the Maddalena. In fact the police went on ahead and we followed them round. When they finally gave up, we returned to our usual haunts.

In all these alarms my one concern was that I might be caught and forced to reveal my identity in front of my companions. And *their* great fear was of being driven to the police station and kept there for a useless and annoying twenty-four hours.

The police could not do otherwise. It was their only way of making sure that these small vagabonds were not dangerous and that they had not already given trouble. They rounded up the boys only to catch those who had run away from home or against whom there had already been some police-charge. And when after twenty-four hours they were proved to be merely *scugnizzi*, they would be released.

There was no institute, no government-subsidised shelter for them, and they could not be kept in jail because they had committed no known crime. Several of my young friends had been arrested and released from twenty to thirty times and had by now become so familiar to the police that they were left alone.

One sergeant—the boys had nicknamed him "Iron Moustaches"—was a good-natured man who knew all of us individually, and there was no harm in him at all providing that you did not try to pull his leg, but there were many others so delighted with their petty authority that they only knew how to make themselves unpleasant. With such as these you could do no more than bow your head and take to your heels before the blows fell.

We once saw a boy—and it was in the middle of the square in front of the railway station—beaten up and flung into a police van like a bundle of rags. The bystanders were horrified and we, watching wretchedly from a distance, were unable to interfere. Later on when we passed another police officer in the Maddalena district—a decent, mild-looking fellow who seemed more than anything like an honest family-man returning tired from his work—he was of course greeted with a barrage of cat-calls, boos and hisses which his colleagues had earned for him. And having expressed their opinion of the police-force in general the *scugnizzi* evaporated.

On another occasion I had the fright of my life. I was walking with a couple of lads along the railway lines behind the *autostrada* to Pompeii when we were suddenly surprised by a guard. We tried to escape by sliding down a steep slope, while he shouted at us to stop. Hearing the click of his rifle "at the ready" we did stop. And I was nearest to him.

He wanted to know all about me. I was not alone now, as I was with that nightwatchman, and I could tell him nothing.

Repeatedly he struck at my legs with his rifle-butt. Have you ever stumbled over a chair and hurt your shin-bone? Can you imagine what it is like to have it hit again and again with a hard piece of wood, deliberately and mercilessly?

I could not speak. I tried to think of Materdei. I was doubled up in agony.

The guard dragged me off like a sack to his barracks, while his fellow guards rounded up the other two. As soon as I could manage a word I said that I wanted to talk to some-body alone.

"*Alone?* Why?"

Then I murmured that I had special information to give them. Their ears are always ready for "special information."

In that small, stark inner office I told them that I was a priest and that I had documents to prove it. They crumbled. Some of them had even heard of me. They did not know what to do to make amends. The one who had hit me put out his hand to me in sympathy and I flinched away from him. After such pain you do that instinctively. Hadn't I seen it in the *scugnizzi*? And wasn't I a *scugnizzo* myself?

But I was also a priest as they now knew, and with unhappy and repentant eyes they let me go.

My companions could not understand it. Why were we all released? As I limped with them back into Naples they wanted to know what had happened.

It was still not time to tell them in full. Perhaps they thought I had been punished enough for all of us. But at least, for a night's rest, I managed to bring them back with me to Materdei.

Two more. Pasquale would shoot me.

*   *   *   *

Oh, how difficult Materdei became at this time! Not only was there this question of bills mounting and my longing to take over the administration of the whole project, but there was this extremely awkward situation of my being in two camps at once. Pasquale and his helpers knew me as Don Mario Borrelli. And their *scugnizzi* knew me as O Naso Stuorto. It was a false situation, I was torn in two, and I longed for the time when they could all think of me as one person. How could it ever happen?

Unforeseen help came from our parish church—the community published a little paper called *Il Granellino*, a simple two-page folder, and it was agreed that one of Salvatore's photographs, showing me with the gang, should be included. This would give me exactly what I needed—faced with this, and with me as a priest, these *scugnizzi* would be able to identify me at last.

But it was too soon. Something happened, on the very same night that I heard the news, which sent me back into the alleys.

It was a stupid indiscretion.

Several *scugnizzi* used to loiter in the sacristy, feeling by now thoroughly at home and enjoying the friendliness of the priests of Materdei. There would be also a few young men from Catholic Youth organisations who knew of my work and used to address me, even when they saw me in rags, as "Father". All very well when there were no *scugnizzi* present, but on this night one of them forgot.

"Oh, Father Borrelli—"

The *scugnizzi* turned their heads, but I was already half-way up the stairs to my room. I shut myself in, exasperated, and paced up and down, trying to restore my nerves. The fool! Two words, and he could have ruined my work. This was not the way to go about things. Once or twice I listened at the door—would they never go? But finally there was silence, and I crept downstairs and rushed out into the night—down the Fontanelle and away into the heart of Naples.

I would have to reveal myself soon, I knew, if only to avoid further incidents of this kind; but before I did so I was going to cast that net still wider. I must make one last effort.

The boys of the Vasto district had thinned out, the station square was almost deserted, and at first I could not think why. Then I heard that they were beginning to join another gang, older and more depraved, masters of all the arts that the pavements could teach them. At the head of them was one called Ciccillo, a tramway-worker, and they haunted the San Carlo Theatre and the huge Galleria Umberto, opposite, where there were so many exploitable tourists lingering at the cafés or staring in shop windows or simply strolling through the vast station-like edifice.

A good hunting-ground, I must say : and I confess that that night I was nervous. The younger *scugnizzi* I knew and had already tackled, but these were, so to speak, war-veterans, a far tougher brood who had explored every possible aspect of life while I was still in the seminary. I was at a loss with them before I had even begun. I had no idea how to approach them : I did not know their terms : I would have to act entirely by instinct. I only hoped I could join the gang without provoking a quarrel.

It took me a little while to find their hide-out. Around a small fire a few young tramps had already settled down on straw-bedding (they seemed to be well-organised in these superior circles.) I lit a cigarette-butt and approached the fire. Eyes were turned to me : I nodded, but there was no response. The faces were hostile, although one or two of them seemed familiar to me.

I could sense the atmosphere and the reason for it. These of course were the "élite" of the *scugnizzo* world, experienced parasites who claimed as their rightful prey the richer foreigners and the well-known opera singers and ballet dancers of the San Carlo. No wonder they were resentful. Being as expert as they were, they could not possibly afford to have some unknown amateur joining them—somebody who through inexperience or recklessness could involve them with the police. It was quite evident that any addition to this gang would be by recommendation.

But I had no credentials to offer: I just stood there, a newcomer. At last a figure arose from a pile of straw, slow and menacing.

"You," he said. "Who are you and what d'you want?"

"Only a bit of fire."

"There's fires all over Naples. Why pick on ours?"

"Well, somebody told me I could sleep here."

"Who told you?"

"Can't remember."

"I'll give you something to remember," said Ciccillo, and he kicked and cuffed me out of the Galleria.

Not the first occasion on which I had known physical pain, but this time I was determined not to show that I minded it: so I sat down on the steps opposite the San Carlo Theatre where they could still see me. I looked at the streets. A boot-black had even at this hour found somebody's shoes to polish. American sailors passed, five of them. A prostitute lingered, turned her head, and then went on towards the Via Roma. There was a crazy jumble of cars at the corner, everybody wanting to go in different and conflicting directions and nobody willing to give way. And then, white and grey, the theatre's neo-classical façade, a stately portico under which there were posters advertising performances of Aida.

It was humiliating, but in the end I had to get up and go, knowing that that night I had failed completely.

* * * *

I told Salvatore about *Il Granellino* and we looked through some of the photographs he had taken months before.

"What we need is a good one of the gang, with of course the extra member."

"But I thought you'd roped most of them in."

"Well, yes—we've got quite a lot of them at Materdei."

"Then we'd better have some new photographs, hadn't we? Or don't you want any more *scugnizzi*? I can't believe you've piled them up to the roof."

"No, there's still plenty of room. And still plenty of *scugnizzi*."

"All right, we start again. Where are you now, anyway?"

For a moment I hesitated; but Salvatore was a friend to whom you did not mind admitting defeat.

"I'm trying to join the San Carlo gang, And I'm not finding it at all easy."

Salvatore's eyebrows rose above his spectacles.

"That little bunch. There's some brute who works on the tramways—"

"Ciccillo. D'you know him?"

"Not yet. But I've heard of his gang and I believe it's the toughest in Naples. How will you manage to get in?"

"I don't know!" Then I added, rashly: "But I shall, tomorrow night."

*   *   *   *

It seemed to me to be the same traffic-jam, as though it had not been able to move since the night before, but perhaps this was always happening. Touts were trying to sell the usual wrist-watches, cameos and "Parker" pens. The boot-black could not find a customer and was banging his box with a stick to attract attention. Tourists, slung with cameras, were walking up the steps into the vaulted brilliantly-lit Galleria with its cafés and shops and there was a queue outside the cinema. There was the same cold white queue along the classical frieze of the San Carlo portico, and posters still promised Aida.

So much as usual, but when I got to the gang's head-quarters I had a shock. Salvatore was already there. Salvatore was talking to everybody. Salvatore was on ex-cellent terms with them.

But hadn't he told me, only yesterday, that he had never met them? Then what on earth could have happened?

It dawned on me then that Salvatore was the perfect neutral. A plain, slightly rotund middle-class Neapolitan with spectacles, he was just an honest citizen but one who obviously knew his way about. From the *scugnizzo* point of view not worth robbing or leading up any sort of garden-path : nor, at the other end of the scale, was he to be feared as a possible rival or a potential danger. He was just what he was, and nobody minded a joke with him.

He had done this for me, knowing that he could make headway with them, secure in his solid immunity. I had to move closer to hear what he was saying. I put one foot against the wall and leant back.

"The *Reverendo*—"

"You mean Don Vesuvio? That priest? Yes, we've heard of his place . . . Mirello"—Ciccillo called to one of the youngest—"didn't you go there once?"

The boy looked down.

"Yes."

"What was it like?"

"Well—I got something to eat—and I got a bed—"

A bright flash. Salvatore.

"All for nothing?"

"Yes."

I sat down beside them.

"Where d'you get hold of this fellow?"

"*He* knows him" said Salvatore pointing to me. "He knows Don Vesuvio."

Faces turned in my direction. Another flash.

"Listen," said Ciccillo, annoyed, "what are you doing, taking photographs? You get money out of them, do you?"

"Nothing," said Salvatore. "Not one *lira*. They're just for my album. And I'm going to take one more."

"You," said Ciccillo to me, "you're the one I kicked out of the place the other night, aren't you?"

"That's right."

"I didn't realise you knew this Don Vesuvio."

Flash.

"I know him well."

"What's he like?"

I shrugged.

"Want to meet him?"

"I wouldn't mind. Bring him along tomorrow."

But I felt entitled to raise difficulties.

"Tomorrow, no. Nor the day after." I was trying to remember when *Il Granellino* was published. "Not until Saturday."

"All right, then, Saturday. You'll bring him?"

"If I can be here," I said, "I'll have him with me."

"And what's your name?"

"Naso Stuorto."

"Believe I've heard that before" said Ciccillo. "Perhaps I've met somebody who knows you."

O Naso Stuorto. Il Reverendo. Don Vesuvio. It was indeed high time that they all became Don Mario Borrelli of Naples.

*   *   *   *

This was the week before Easter, and what a wonderful time that is in our city! We all become far more Neapolitan than we ever were before: it is as though an electric current were suddenly switched on. In every alley, on every battered flight of steps in the slums, in every courtyard or square or obscure corner, there is a shrine which perhaps you had never noticed before. It is now lovingly lit, it is draped with clean brocades and tinsel, and in front of it there are early carnations and sweet-scented stocks and irises and anemones and lilies. Everybody sits out of doors in the evening, there are children about, there is much conversation and laughter, and good wishes are called out to neighbours or passers-by. Somewhere the sauce for *pasta* smells very tempting. Somewhere there is, of course, music. Chairs and people are silhouetted against golden doorways, and the light turns the cheap street flags above you into splendid bànners.

All districts vie with one another in their Easter display —our little alley must be no less beautiful than yours. In the main streets, and even in smaller ones, shopkeepers have spent hours in trying to amuse or charm or distract you. This is a time of pride.

It is also for the Neapolitan people a time of arrogance. On the Thursday before Easter there is the ancient ceremony of *lo struscio*—down one of our busiest streets, the Via Roma, people shuffle. They shuffle, they do not walk. Walking would be quite impossible because there are too many of them. They are all over the road, and no traffic can possibly get through. No traffic tries. Slowly, slowly they shuffle, greeting one another and stopping to talk. The streets and the roads are theirs. Yes, this is the time of arrogance.

There is also a time of devotion. From one church to another—and how many churches are there in Naples?— the families go to gape with wonder at the Easter altars and their varieties of decoration. The yellow and the gold, the red and the twinkling candelabra—where did they all come from? A time of wonder and devotion and silence.

On Thursday *lo struscio*. On Friday the church. Then on Saturday *Il Granellino*—if it ever came out in time!— with the best of those photographs on the front cover. It would be the first Saturday in ages on which I did not need to change my cassock for rags.

Salvatore and I went to the Galleria early in the evening with a copy of the paper. I was afraid that it might be even too early and that the gang would not be there—but I had to attend the Easter midnight service and I was forced to watch the clock.

A priest. But my clothes did not make any difference to my feelings, for I had been a priest and a *scugnizzo* the whole time. I was merely myself.

It was not too early; a few of them were there, though not all. Salvatore gave them cigarettes and introduced me as "Don Vesuvio." They obviously did not recognise me. I smiled at them and then kept quiet, letting him talk.

"Well," he said, handing them the copy of *Il Granellino*, "here you all are."

Even though *scugnizzi* who have been in contact with the police may be frightened of photographs there is a certain vanity in all Neapolitans which makes them delight in seeing themselves in black and white.

"That's me!" cried O Mirello.

"And me," said Zucculetta. "Look, Mimi, there's you and O Scugnato—"

"But who's that?" Salvatore was pointing at my own image, at a creature in rags. "D'you know him?"

"Just a minute," said Paperino. "There's O Maritiello, and then . . . no, I don't know that one."

"Give it me," said Ciccillo. "I'll tell you who it is." He looked at the paper. "That's the one I kicked out of the Galleria. That's the one who was here last week. What did he say his name was—O Naso Stuorto? He said he was going to bring that priest along." He looked at me. He faltered. He glanced back at the photograph, then back at me. Then he said: "Is that *you* . . . Father?"

"Yes, I'm Don Vesuvio and I'm O Naso Stuorto. I'm both."

There was a pause. It seemed a long one. They needed

time to understand. Then suddenly I was nearly knocked over, I was invaded by *scugnizzi*. They pulled at my clothes, they tried to kiss me, they clung to my hands. I wasn't prepared for this. They were young toughs—but then they were also Neapolitans. They knew that what I had done I had done with love, and they knew instinctively, though they could never have said it, that that was what they most needed.

With ludicrous inappropriateness four garishly dressed trumpeters came on to the portico of the San Carlo Theatre and blew a clarion-call into the night, to advertise Aida.

The *scugnizzi* were still clinging to me. I tried to look at Salvatore and perhaps he tried to look at me—but how could we possibly hope to see one another?

CHAPTER EIGHTEEN

Two Shadows

You cannot expect to know the *scugnizzo* without knowing also his companions of the night. That "spinning top" travels a crazy path through the underworld of Naples, and in order to understand him completely you must understand the people with whom he associates—those with whom his risky and precarious livelihood is inevitably linked —the pickpocket, the pimp, ponce and procurer, the forger of false identity cards, and the woman under the street-lamp.

All these people are in some way related: their interests merge, overlap, and are so confused that in their preying on society they are sometimes forced to prey on one another.

In the sinister darkness of their commerce the *scugnizzo* is sometimes an enthusiastic helper. Often they need him as much as he needs them. He saves them trouble. If he does not happen to know the right "contacts", he finds them. He is indispensable. He has learnt that most people in the world need assistance, without ever realising that he needs it more than anyone else.

Well, there are shady characters in every large city, but I wonder where else than in a busy and ancient port like Naples you will find little boys of no age at all touting for prostitutes, pulling drunken sailors by the elbow and propelling them from the rear, as though they were some wonderful cargo that had been washed up in the gulf, shouting up to them obscenities in languages which I wish I did not understand, and making gestures that are only too obvious.

Let me be frank. As a priest—and indeed before I had ever been to a Seminary—I was always disgusted by those women who look at the money rather than at the man. No body was ever made for such a mechanical, calculated degradation.

I have not changed my opinion, but inevitably, changing my outlook on the world, I have found myself in the disguise of a tired and tattered *scugnizzo* sitting down by one of our bucket fires in the winter, or on a doorstep in the summer, and talking at length to such poor raddled streetwomen as came into our lane; talking to them as one human being to another.

And I can no longer judge them. Let me try to understand them. They have much to teach me in terms of human behaviour, and I am always on the verge of an abyss into which I am afraid to look : but I must look all the same if I am to know. And perhaps the light will be all the greater for the dark.

Nannina was one of these women, at the street corner or leaning on a wall, smiling under a doorway or an arch or at a reflection in a shop window, or strolling with decreasing hopefulness on the edge of the pavement. She was probably no more than twenty-five years old, but of course looked a great deal older. Suffering, pain and mortification, combined with the need to attract, had made her almost grotesque—a soft red grin in a chalk-white face and eyes like burnt holes in a blanket. And yet in spite of this one could see beauty there. The lines were still good—the forehead and nose and chin—a sudden turn of the head or a moment of stillness and you could forget the years, the pain, the pretence.

I knew her story; and I wish it were not such a familiar one, that of the peasant girl whose family has discovered that she had been seduced and left.

Here in Italy that creates an impossible situation at once. The family—consisting not only of parents but of uncles and aunts and brothers and sisters and cousins and nieces and nephews—in fact, a large proportion of the village—is at once outraged and betrayed by the discovery, and the neighbours gossip endlessly. No man will ever dream of marrying her. People do not look up at her from their stitching or straw-plaiting when she passes, and they turn back from their windows and balconies. Even children are silent, having overheard the remarks of their elders. She walks alone, poor girl, except for this grinning ghost of shame that is with her wherever she goes, tapping her on the shoulder. At table all are silent, and she takes her bowl, crying, into the backyard among the hens. It is a nightmare.

More than that, it is intolerable. Even for a moderately sophisticated adult it would be impossible to bear, but a country girl is completely defenceless in the face of so big a problem. The little that she knew of life has been overshadowed by the fact that this is what has happened to her in her brief journey through adolescence.

What can she do? Escape by killing herself? Or by submerging herself in a big city like Naples—where she can make a living only by offering her body? Offering nightly for men's use the body that she once gave to a soldier who told her beforehand that he loved her and only afterwards that he was married?

I ask you, how can you be clear and rational and dogmatic about such problems? Can you possibly know how anyone should have behaved at any given moment?

Well, that was Nannina's story, or part of it. The rest was even less romantic. As a street-walker she was arrested by the police. Not being a Neapolitan herself, and therefore not listed as a "professional"—a degree of respectability, it almost seemed!—she was abruptly ordered back to her village. In other words she was given a *foglio di via*, which technically forbade her to live in Naples.

What was the girl to do? What could they *expect* her to do? They knew perfectly well that she could not possibly go back to a birthplace poisoned by gossip, to the pointing fingers, the averted face, the closed shutter, the slammed door.

In the end the authorities escorted her there, but of course she returned like an arrow and was arrested again. In prison for two months, she went straight back on the streets and—since Naples is a port open to all sailors of all nationalities—contracted syphilis. Again she was arrested, and this time they took her to hospital.

After several months Nannina left there, officially cured—but really, what does that mean? On this particular night, the night when I last talked to her, she was ill again. Young. So young, so used, and with syphilis.

There was at that time a sanitary control of brothels, well for what it was worth, but she would have nothing to do with that. Disgusted by the life of a street-walker she still did not know how to give it up—and yet she was terrified of going back into hospital. She was menaced from all sides, and even from within.

I wonder if you have looked, as I have, at a prostitute trudging the streets all night, bright and hopeful at first, swinging her hips by routine and getting her smile ready at a footfall echoing even in another street. But the night goes on and on and for one reason or another—the weather is too bad or the weather is too good or everybody is listening to the radio—nobody wants her. She searches until she is too tired to search any longer. It is too late, and she is defeated . . .

"Nannina!" She had not noticed me, and my voice surprised her. "Listen, Nannina, not tonight, there's nobody."

"What d'you mean, dear?"

She turned and walked down the lane towards me, and

as somebody unexpectedly switched on a light in a window
I saw her as she was.

"Nobody for you—nobody. You're ill, Nannina, and . . .
well, I'm sorry, but you *look* it. Now be reasonable. Who
d'you suppose—?"

"Oh, I don't know. Leave me alone, could you?"

"Not when you're like this."

She laughed gruffly, wheezily—a voice coarse and deep.

"Like what? Like what I usually am, and I've got to
the stage where you don't get much worse."

The light in the window went out, but I had already seen
enough and was horrified. I put my hand on her arm and
she seemed slightly startled, I don't know why—perhaps the
gestures that she knew far better were not as gentle as mine.

"Do me a favour, will you, Nannina?"

"What sort of a favour, dear?"

"Go home and sleep!"

"*Sleep!*" She jerked back her head and what might have
been laughter turned into a paroxysm of coughing, which
sent her reeling back to the wall.

"That's a good one" she said at last, producing a flimsy
handkerchief from her handbag and dabbing her mouth
gingerly, so as not to disturb her make-up too much. "Sleep,"
she said. "That's a good one, that really is. Listen, dear, it's
in the *daytime* you sleep, not at night. The night's your
money—understand? Well, you can't ignore that, can you?
I mean, it doesn't do. Because—" I saw her lurch slightly
and then recover herself. "Can—can a lady sit down—?"

"Let me recommend a doorstep, Nannina." I sat, trying
to encourage her. "This is a nice one—worn and curved

and friendly, you know what I mean?"

"I do indeed!" She guffawed hoarsely, but still did not follow me as I had hoped she would. I said:

"Can't you ever relax? Why are you standing there? Who d'you think you're waiting for?"

"Prince Charming, didn't you know?" I dismissed this as cheap irony until I heard her say: "I thought I'd found him once. But that was a few years back."

"Not so many, Nannina?"

"Well, not so many" she said. "No, a few years, just my lifetime." She turned to me, momentarily beaten by looking back, and said, as though in sudden panic, "Look, if I do sit down will you help me to get up again?"

"Of course!"

In Naples a doorstep can be a welcome seat. I shifted my place. *Senza complimenti*, and you don't stand on ceremony. And so Nannina at last sat down beside me, slowly and obviously afraid of her own tiredness. Afraid that she might be there forever.

"Nice," she said suddenly. "It's nice sitting down and talking to a friend, and I'll tell you something, dear. You won't believe it at all, not from a woman whose job it is to keep company the whole time, but it's true all the same. You can take my word for it, you get *lonely*. Just lonely. As for love, why, you're everybody's and nobody's."

"If you're everybody's and nobody's, Nannina, don't let's call that love."

"Anybody'd think you were a preacher," she said crossly. "And anyway nobody's got any right to tell *me* what's what." She put her head in her hands and I could hear her breathing heavily, and I knew that when she talked again I must not interrupt her.

"All right, I sell it, so that means it isn't love. So I don't know what love is, do I? I probably don't and I never shall now, but once I thought I did and I got caught out. He said he loved me and I wanted him and I also wanted a family—doesn't that sound funny?—a whole row of *bambini* pulling the place to bits. I wouldn't have cared where the place was or what it was. I'd have been happy." Her hand went up in a gesture of one, two, three: children, in stages. "But then there was the trial."

"The trial, Nannina? You never told me."

"Oh, I don't mean a *real* trial, not in a court of law. Their own trial of me, I meant, the way they treated me . . . and that's why I came here. No, when I come to think of it now, if anybody was on trial it wasn't me. It was—"

"*La gente.*"

"Yes, it was people, and they don't look very good, not from this doorstep. People! Excuse me—" she spat vigorously —"why, it's just people that's made me what I am. Who's driven me into this but people? And crazy, isn't it? People don't want me to be a tart, I disgrace them. So people force me into being one. So people give me their diseases. So they force me into hospital. So I come out. So I get them again." The wet sardonic grin was painful. "It's people, dear, just people, and I can't fight them any more because I'm tired."

"Then if you're tired, why don't you—"

"Listen," she said, with a sudden show of defiance. "Get me up on my feet will you?" I helped her rise from the doorstep. "That's better." She was full of bravado as though she had instantly regretted admitting her weakness.

"You need somebody to protect you."

"What a chance, dear, with my profession written on my face as clearly as if it had been tattooed, and walking the way I do."

"Wouldn't you be better off in a house?"

"A *house*?" She laughed bitterly, and her laughter turned into a fit of coughing. "You ask," she wheezed, "because you just don't know." She turned those dark sockets towards me. "That's a fine thing, a whore-shop, I've been in one. Three quarters of your earnings, that's what they take. *Three quarters*! And once you get into their clutches you've little chance of getting out of them. Besides—you've got to do just what they want—or rather, what their clients want, and sometimes you get clients with very peculiar ideas. You're not allowed to refuse them, you know, not in a house. You've got to do anything and everything. It's no good minding what you do."

"But surely—if you're on the streets that's the way things are anyhow? It must be just the same thing, but without the protection?"

"No," she said. "No, you're wrong. On the streets you can refuse if you want, but in a house you daren't. And as for protection—what sort of protection are you talking about, dear?"

"Medical."

"Oh, that!" She grinned wryly. "And a lot of good it does. A bit more useful, I think, if they checked *the men who came in*, though I must say, that'd keep them busy. As

194

things are, how's a man to know that the very one before him hadn't got it? As for us women, we keep getting infected and flung out into hospital. The brothel sends us there—but only if they think they can't exploit us in other ways ... Anyhow, I'm far better off as I am. Oh yes, I can pocket my earnings and I don't have to share them, I don't get just one thousand out of every four I've earned. I'm free too, and in a brothel you're fenced in. No going out, nothing like that, you're caged."

Nannina looked round at the looming walls of the alley as though they were green and spacious. And she gave them a momentary smile.

But then she hardened again, for no apparent reason, and her voice was so bitter and cruel that it stung.

"As for diseases—if I get presents of *that* sort—well, I like to pass them on!"

"Oh, Nannina—!"

"It's true." Her face mocked and challenged and was triumphant. This was what people, *la gente*, did to her, so this was what she did to *la gente*. And without the slightest remorse.

She must have noticed the horror on my face, and unfortunately my vulnerability seemed to encourage and even excite her. She delighted in seeing me cornered because I could not bear what she had said. Therefore, as a small part of her revenge on society, she had to repeat it with increasing defiance:

"I like to pass them on! I like to pass them on!"

"Stop shouting, Nannina."

After a moment she said, a little more calmly:

"All right, dear, if you don't want to hear the truth."

We both fell silent and only Naples spoke—the distant trolleybus, two cats, a song on the radio, a quarrel between men outside a wine-shop, a baby whimpering somewhere.

I said at last:

"Nannina—please go home."

She began to laugh. The laughter shook her, filled her, became uncontrollable, and turned into a fit of coughing. Then the coughing too became uncontrollable and I put out my hand to her because I thought she was going to fall down. Her own hand clutched bonily at me and at the same time her eyes, a moment ago dark patches that might have held contempt, derision, even hatred, were anxiously trying to find mine because she was in great need of help. It was a crisis: she was ill, friendless and terrified, and the clawing hand and the burning eyes betrayed her defeat.

From her expression I somehow knew that I had to lead her into a corner, and when I saw the dark red stain down the wall, even black it seemed in that light, I saw too that there was not much left of life for this girl of twenty-five.

La gente had made her too old.

In a little while she was able to lean back on the wall and wipe her lips and breathe again and let her eyes wander to find out where she was. I don't think she saw me for a few minutes: I was somehow out of focus.

I said in my mind, "Nannina, go home to bed!" but it was of no use saying it again out loud.

Crumpled in my pocket was the modest bundle of *lire* that schoolteaching had brought me that week—little indeed compared with what Nannina herself, had she been well, and had it been even a few months ago, could have earned in far less time. Such are the values of mankind that we could not possibly compete.

Small as the sum was, I gave it her. Perhaps she would understand and go home, she would not need to fight any longer? For a day or two, there would be a respite? I pulled at the pocket of that loose swinging coat and put the money in : and as I walked away from her I knew through the back of my head that she was taking it out and looking at it in astonishment.

"But why?"

I went on in my clumsy boots towards the end of the lane and the night's mainstream of the Via Roma, and before I had gone far I heard her say again :

"Why? But *why* did you do this?"

And perhaps her voice was, for the first time that night, the voice of a woman.

*   *   *   *

Now I must describe to you another shadow—smaller, and a very different one, and yet not unrelated to that of Nannina. Indeed, as I have said already, the life of the *scugnizzo* is sometimes bound up with that of the prostitute. He may tout for her, and for his offices is sometimes rewarded by an hour or two in her bed, after all clients have gone. Which I regret to say may land him, at a very early age, in hospital.

Not that that can possibly have been the case with Carluc-ciello. No, surely he was too young.

I cannot talk of the child immediately. No, I must talk of other things first in order to reach him. He's difficult to catch, as he always was.

It happened in April, I remember, about the middle of the month in which our skies become kinder and the air more caressing, and when the sea begins to ripple into a smile. Oh how much spirit there is in the sea of Naples, and how much sea in the Neapolitan spirit! In our songs, too; they sound like the sea and are drenched with it. We are a sea-people, we dream of it and breathe with it and in our wakeful hours we turn our heads towards it. We eat its varied, many-coloured creatures with delight, whenever and how often we can. (I myself, who eat practically nothing else but fish, have been known to say "Oh I'm so glad it's Friday again!")

The sea, the Neapolitan sea. If you go up to the museum of S. Martino to look at very early pictures of Naples, you will find that they were all of them painted from the sea. It is inseparable from us. Every Neapolitan thinks of the sea as another member of his family.

And every *scugnizzo* is half a sea-creature—I do not mean only the water-boys of Santa Lucia diving for coins, but the real *scugnizzo*, from whatever part of Naples. He belongs to the sea, and its many caprices seem to echo his own. It can be quiet, generous, amicable, as he can, it can laugh, it can beckon, it can be turbulent and aggressive, it can be viciously cruel. Its abrupt changes of mood seem to him perfectly understandable. He is a friend of the sea—and sometimes, alas, the sea seems to be his only friend.

He goes down to it constantly, and in mild weather he

will be driven by instinct to sleep on the rocks beside it, lulled by its sound and perhaps with one hand flung down to it in welcome.

The *scugnizzo* has many sorrows—which is indeed the reason why he is a *scugnizzo*—and with that hand trailing in the water he is confiding them to a friend.

And so Carlucciello went down to the sea.

I had seen him many times and knew that in some way he was different from the others. What do I mean by that? It is difficult to define, but those who have ever dealt with children will know how subtly but unmistakably one child can put a ring round himself, even without meaning to do so.

Why does he separate himself not only from us but from other children? Is he an accusation, a sort of reproach to humanity? I wish I knew.

The purely physical things that distinguished Carlucciello were that he was painfully thin, and that for some reason he was perpetually running—his fine hair streaming in the wind. He was the statue of a young Mercury in fact, though it would be difficult to think of Carlucciello as anything as immobile as a statue. No, let me change Mercury to quicksilver itself, the liquid elusive metal. That is how he always was: and if we can return to a sea-image I think of him as a bright flashing eel leaping from your hand and not to be recovered.

Forcibly interrupted or cornered, he could, before escaping, show fight. Bold and angry and bruised too much, he would spit abuse and be off like an arrow, a fugitive from hurt.

I remember once watching him on the shore of Santa Lucia, not far from the Restaurant Zi' Teresa, and fortunately he did not see me at all. His eyes were only for the sea. The sea was tickling his chin with its light and there was a glow under his cheekbones. His lips were parted. He was hypnotised. It seemed to me that he was even breathing in the rhythm of the boats at anchor.

And then for the first time I saw him smile, as though he were greeting a friend.

Why didn't I realise then that the friendship would be a fatal one—why didn't I know that the sea's embrace would be too strong for him?

Or was that what he wanted?

Let me state it simply: a small boy was drowned off the rocks of Santa Lucia, and was washed up as white as the gulls above him.

These are the bare facts, but what a fuss the newspapers made about them!

Why, I wonder? Journalists who ordinarily did not care if *scugnizzi* lived or died wrote stirring, even heartrending articles on the subject of Carlucciello—perhaps no film-star was being re-married that week, the gangsters were taking a holiday, no more embezzlements had come to light, America and Russia were reasonably quiet and there was really very little to say. So the boy stole the limelight. It grew stronger and stronger. Like dogs howling in the night, one journalist set off another, and in the end Carlucciello's poor little body received what might in some circles be called an excellent press.

The sea, of course, was the villain of the piece—they had

to supply an abstract villain, in order to prevent their readers from wondering who was really to blame. Not a word about social conditions, but Father Neptune in the doghouse—this lad snatched by the sea as some kind of sacrifice! Really, some of the articles were so nauseating as to be unreadable. Then—since nothing more interesting had yet occurred to titillate the public taste—the subject had to be stretched and stretched, until one could have almost hoped that some important conclusion might have been reached. We all waited for it. And it arrived at last.

Vigilance was needed! Really, little boys sleeping on those rocks in the mild weather (though indeed *why* did they when they must have had homes to go to?) must be protected. *The conscience of Naples demanded it!* (Only this?)

In the concrete forests of bureaucracy a plastic bird began to sing, and this is what we heard. In token of Carlucciello's drowning—almost, it seemed, in celebration of it—half a regiment of coast-watchers was detailed to watch the coast.

This wicked sea must not steal any other child of Naples.

Not even if he wants to be stolen.

You will ask me now if I think Carlucciello really meant to kill himself, to die in the arms of the only friend he knew, and I can only tell you that it seems to me most unlikely. It is not in the nature of any Neapolitan to commit suicide, we love life far too much. And yet—I confess I do not know what horrors that boy had seen, or what he had had to endure that day.

People asked one another, as Neapolitans always do whenever some child is involved in an accident: "Whose is he?

Whom does he belong to?" Not realising of course that he belonged to every one of us. That child was ours, yours, mine and theirs.

Of no use to look at the newspapers. They said nothing even about his home, if he had one or if it could be called one, and they had not bothered to trace his mother. It is really surprising that with such a dearth of sensational topics they had not been driven by necessity into trying to understand the problem. But suddenly Carlucciello was dropped.

It was a relief to me, because I could not bear what they said about him. Now, some really unsavoury carcass was caught in the net of publicity, and it would obviously take them some time to digest it.

Carlucciello was, after all, merely a *scugnizzo*. And a little while later there were no longer any coast-watchers watching the coast . . .

Now, unlike the journalists, let us open a door without being afraid of what we shall find behind it.

Rusella is a woman of thirty-six, looking like her own grandmother, dry, wrinkled, with withered and pendulous breasts. This is her home, and it was once Carlucciello's—a fetid, squalid cave measuring about six foot six by eight foot long. There is room for only one bed, which of course has to be used as chair and table too : it is everything and it is all that they have, this family bed. At night there are no less than five people between its stained and sordid sheets. And there Rusella sits rocking herself to and fro, half-demented by grief and remorse and remembering Carlucciello.

He was one of those *scugnizzi* born in utter poverty, and

the others in his cave had flung him out to pick up a living for himself. If that sounds unbearably cruel, please do remember the conditions of a home like that, and think how they can corrupt all reason and all sense of humanity. Do you suppose that any Neapolitan mother would want to lose her child? For Carlucciello on his own, things *might* be better: at home they could not be worse: that was the argument. And so he went to his freedom and to his death.

The bitterness of her remorse is only too evident—and yet she is not to blame for what has happened, not Rusella. I can tell you who were culpable, and there are many of them.

You Christians who watch the world and its sorrows through your windows, who talk of moral corruption and do nothing practical to prevent it—you had a hand in killing him; and you too who are so comfortably rich that the knowledge of poverty is beyond you and the thought of it disgusting. The authorities too were responsible with their ingrown apathy, their stupid frustrating concern with useless detail and forms that must be filled in, filed and forgotten—to say nothing of their assumed ignorance of those who are so obviously embezzling funds intended for charity!

If all of these killed him—then I did too. Oh, why didn't I start my work years and years before? Why so squeamish about putting on rags and sleeping on newspaper and enduring the alley-boys' vermin? Long ago, though I am still young, I could have started collecting the children of Naples and building a house for them—if needs be with my own hands, and certainly with my heart.

*   *   *   *

I gave you one reason for combining in a single chapter two portraits—one of a prostitute and the other of a child.

But there is a second reason.

Among the many ghosts of Naples, Nannina's is a sudden white face at every street corner, turning at the sound of a footfall.

And as for Carlucciello, I am carrying him in my arms forever, a boy only nine years old.

CHAPTER NINETEEN

Hands
Wanted

There is more to say, of course : there always is. Some things I have seen and known I shall carry with me, in silence, to my grave. I refuse to write of them; I do not want sensationalism. The truths I have already told you are quite sensational enough.

This is not a book of statistics either. If I say that my *scugnizzi*—they have become yours too, I hope—are now being taught five different trades, and that Swiss charity has given us five thousand pounds' worth of machinery for their engineering course—that is splendid news. It is splendid too that another *Casa* is to be built. But these things do not touch the core of the problem nor the heart of my story.

I could add that many have emigrated successfully, to England, Switzerland, America and even Argentina, and that many have found good work in Italy. And I could also add something which you have already guessed—that there have been failures too. These can hurt, but they can never dismay or discourage me. Even if they were numerous, what would they matter in comparison with one ragged little unloved thief taken out of the gutter and turned into a well-integrated and decent member of society?

That does not happen overnight. It is a long process. Sometimes I have found them at the age of seven : sometimes they have left me at twenty-one. After they have gone, I can no longer watch over them. The rest is up to you.

Sometimes I think that this is not only an autobiography but the story of a human factory in which the crudest of raw material becomes transformed. And as many factories do, I would like to put up a notice saying : HANDS WANTED.

I would like to put it up not only on Materdei but all over the world.

For only with help can the street lamp meet the stars.

PUBLISHER'S NOTE

We would like to inform readers of this book that a Fund has been started in Britain supporting the work of Father Mario Borrelli of the *Casa Dello Scugnizzo* in Naples. Readers wishing to help the Fund may send contributions to : The House of the Urchins Fund, Midland Bank, 69 Pall Mall, London, S.W.1.